Intermediate Sanctions

NONPROFIT LAW, FINANCE, AND MANAGEMENT SERIES

Intermediate Sanctions

Curbing Nonprofit Abuse

BRUCE R. HOPKINS
D. BENSON TESDAHL

John Wiley & Sons, Inc.

New York • Chichester • Weinheim • Brisbane • Singapore • Toronto

Library of Congress Cataloging in Publication Data:

ISBN 0-471-17456-4

Printed in the United States of America

10 9 8 7 6 5 4 3 2 1

To my dear wife, Bonnie J. Buchele,
in appreciation for her enthusiastic
support and interest in this project
(thereby becoming one of the few
psychologists in the nation knowing
something about intermediate sanctions).

BRH

To my wife Linda, with love, and to my mentor,
Bruce Hopkins, with gratitude for sharing
with me his vast knowledge of the law of
tax-exempt organizations.

DBT

About the Authors

Bruce R. Hopkins is a lawyer in Kansas City, Missouri, having practiced law in Washington, DC, for 26 years. He specializes in the representation of nonprofit organizations. His practice ranges over the entirety of legal matters involving nonprofit organizations, including issues pertaining to the application of intermediate sanctions, and interpretation of the private inurement and private benefit doctrines.

Mr. Hopkins has served as Chair of the Committee on Exempt Organizations, Tax Section, American Bar Association; Chair, Section of Taxation, National Association of College and University Attorneys; and President, Planned Giving Study Group of Greater Washington, DC. He was accorded the Assistant Commissioner's (IRS) Award in 1984. He also teaches a course on nonprofit organizations at the University of Missouri—Kansas City School of Law.

Mr. Hopkins is the series editor of Wiley's Nonprofit Law, Finance, and Management Series. In addition to *Intermediate Sanctions: Curbing Nonprofit Abuse*, he is the author of *The Legal Answer Book for Nonprofit Organizations; The Law of Tax-Exempt Organizations, Sixth Edition; The Law of Fund-Raising, Second Edition; Charity, Advocacy, and the Law; The Nonprofit Law Dictionary; The Tax Law of Charitable Giving;* and *A Legal Guide to Starting and Managing a Nonprofit Organization, Second Edition;* and is co-author, with Jody Blazek, of *Private Foundations: Tax Law and Compliance,* and with Thomas K. Hyatt, of *The Law of Tax-Exempt Healthcare Organizations.* He also writes *The Nonprofit Counsel,* a monthly newsletter, published by John Wiley & Sons.

Mr. Hopkins earned his J.D. and LL.M. degrees at the George Washington University and his B.A. at the University of Michigan.

D. Benson Tesdahl is a lawyer with Powers, Pyles, Sutter & Verville, P.C., in Washington, DC. He holds a B.S. degree from the U.S. Military

Academy at West Point and an M.S. degree in systems management from the University of Southern California. He earned his J.D. degree from the University of Oregon Law School, where he was elected to the national law school honor society, Order of the Coif, and was an associate editor of the *Oregon Law Review*. He subsequently earned a Master of Laws (LL.M.) degree in taxation, *with distinction*, from Georgetown University.

Mr. Tesdahl specializes in the representation of tax-exempt organizations. His practice includes the establishment and qualification for tax exemption of all types of nonprofit organizations, and advice on such matters as the unrelated business income rules, the use of nonprofit and for-profit subsidiaries, the formation of joint ventures and health care integrated delivery systems, the sale of tax-exempt health care entities, and lobbying and political campaign restrictions. He also advises nonprofit organizations on collateral areas of law, including general corporate law and state charitable fund-raising statutes.

Mr. Tesdahl is an Adjunct Professor of Law at Georgetown University Law Center, where he teaches an advanced seminar on tax-exempt organizations as part of the University's graduate tax program. In addition to numerous published tax articles, he has written chapters for two books on nonprofit organizations published by John Wiley & Sons, Inc. He also writes a monthly tax column for the *Exempt Organization Tax Review*, published by Tax Analysts, and he is the North American Legal Editor for the *Journal of Nonprofit and Voluntary Sector Marketing*, published by Henry Stewart Publications of London, England.

Mr. Tesdahl is a member of the American Bar Association's Committee on Exempt Organizations and the Exempt Organizations Committee of the District of Columbia Bar. He is also co-chair of the ABA Exempt Organizations Subcommittee on Non-501(c)(3) Entities.

Preface

Writing a book about a newly enacted body of law presents certain challenges. One challenge—probably the most obvious—has been reflected in the reactions of many who learned about the book as it was being prepared. Over the past months, we repeatedly heard: "A book about intermediate sanctions! A whole book? What could possibly be said about this subject in a *book?*"

Two rationales are offered for a *book* at this time, other than the need to summarize the new rules on intermediate sanctions. One is to emphasize the importance of the rules to the nonprofit community. A sentence in the book makes this point: "Intermediate sanctions have the promise of transforming the private inurement and private benefit doctrines, and are likely to impact the composition and functioning of many boards of directors of nonprofit organizations" (p. 7).

The other is to stress how much of this body of new law rests on direct precedents: over 70 years of development of the private inurement doctrine, and a quarter-century buildup of the tax law pertaining to private foundations. Most of the organizations that will be caught up in the intermediate sanctions penalties are public charities. Our experience—a combined total of 33 years of practice in the exempt organizations field—is that lawyers and accountants who manage and advise public charities often know little or nothing of private foundation law. Thus, in mastering the panoply and refinements of intermediate sanctions, one must learn much law heretofore unique to private foundations. These elements of that law are summarized in this book.

Another challenge has been the development of a book at this point in time. As lawyers well know, a statutory scheme of law is just the beginning. Usually, that law regime is amplified and informed by a multitude of other law forms, such as regulations, agency rulings, and court opinions. Except for what has accreted in the fields of private inurement, private benefit, and private foundations, no such body of informative law underlies and explains the substance and procedure of intermediate sanctions. Indeed, these sanctions lack even the usual complement of legislative history.

These other law forms will be forthcoming, but they are months away, even as proposals. We are treating the substance and outer edges of this body of law without the benefit of any guidance from the Internal Revenue Service (IRS) and other information sources within the Department of the Treasury.

Intermediate sanctions have been on the brink of enactment for years. We and others in the exempt organizations community have long regarded these sanctions as inevitable. The only mystery—and that was scant—surrounding intermediate sanctions was *when* they would be enacted. Even the effective date of these penalties was known for over a year.

Yet, the Treasury Department did nothing to provide guidance on this new law. What Treasury could have done, or *should* have done, was have an intermediate sanctions package available within one week of enactment of the sanctions—say, by early August of 1996. (A set of guidance documents of suitable length in question-and-answer form would have been ideal.) This did not happen. During the subsequent months, the exempt organizations community has been foundering without guidance as to the workings of these significant new rules. This book is intended as a source of help, at least until some official interpretations of intermediate sanctions emerge.

This intention has offered us still another challenge. We have done what we can to interpret and speculate as to the meaning, range, and direction of this new law. Readers will want to monitor developments in this field and factor them into the material contained in the book.

The greatest challenge will be the intermediate sanctions themselves. Their potential impact on the operations of nonprofit organizations is enormous. Much of the actual outcome will depend on the vigor of the IRS and, ultimately, of the courts. Also to be considered is the extent to which public charities and social welfare organizations will take steps either to avoid benefit transactions with disqualified persons or to adequately document the case that excess benefit is not involved. One aspect of the emergence of these new rules is certain (and this should be a not-particularly-subtle tip-off for the management of nonprofit organizations): intermediate sanctions will significantly augment the practices of lawyers and accountants in the tax-exempt organizations field.

We wish to extend our heartfelt thanks to those who worked so hard to help us publish this book on a "fast track" basis: Martha Cooley and Mary Daniello at John Wiley & Sons, Inc., and Nancy Marcus Land and Maryan Malone of Publications Development Company. We have worked with each of them in the past and—as always—it is a delightful experience.

BRUCE R. HOPKINS
D. BENSON TESDAHL

March 1997

Contents

Surprises in Store

Jack Dunlop paced restlessly behind his desk, deep into a Friday afternoon. His attention was repeatedly drawn to the office windows, beyond which the bright sun caressed the landscape, causing his thoughts to converge on his golf game. When his tee-off time was less than an hour away, Jack, as chief executive officer of a tax-exempt, charitable hospital, received the institution's just-completed annual return, which was to be filed with the IRS on the following Monday. Anxious to leave for the day, it was all Jack could do to give the pages of the document a cursory review. However, when he came to the portion of the return that listed the compensation of the five highest paid employees of the hospital, he paused, pleased at what he saw. Alongside his name, at the top of the list, was annual compensation of $300,000. Jack felt validated by this achievement; his image of his worth was enhanced by the level of his remuneration. He scrawled his signature across the return, dated it for the coming Monday, and left his office. As he drove to the golf course, Jack felt exhilarated.

Betty McGowan took pride in her work as director of one of the region's largest museums. Its fine collections, arrayed throughout several buildings, had earned the museum a widespread reputation. Betty was a stickler for details, and her passion for accuracy carried over to her responsibility for reviewing and signing the museum's return, which had to be filed annually with the IRS. Betty was pleased with this year's return, believing it faithfully portrayed the institution's program and finances. Betty was not formally trained in the preparation of financial statements, however, and so her eyes passed lightly over the page of the return where it was reported that a parcel of real

1

estate, on which the newest of the museum's buildings had been constructed, was being rented to the museum. The landlord was a partnership; the partners were Betty, her husband, her stepbrother, and her stepbrother's wife. Her scan of the page triggered Betty's admission that her stepbrother had worked quite a deal, leasing the property to the museum for an annual rent of $700,000. He had told her later that the true rental value of the property was probably less than $500,000. Betty comforted herself by rationalizing that the museum was still benefiting from the transaction.

Howard McKenzie, the president of a small private college, was completing another hectic week in academia. He was looking forward to a few days of rest, reading, and contemplation. Howard disliked forms, he disliked numbers, and he certainly disliked the IRS, but he could no longer shirk the task that had to be completed that very day: the review and signing of the college's annual return. He plodded through the pages, wishing that the return was not so extensive and the government's questions were not so pointed. But Howard's energy level surged when he came to the list of the college's highest paid employees. There he was; his earned annual compensation of $250,000 was second only to the football coach. Renewed stamina propelled Howard through the rest of the return. Thinking that the envy of his colleagues was assured and his station in higher education was secure, Howard signed the return with a flourish and departed for the weekend with confidence.

Mary Adams was finishing her day as executive director of an advocacy group. As founder of the organization and its only chief executive, Mary was proud of its influence and the respect it engendered from those who were lobbied. The group was only in its sixth year of operation, but it was, in her estimation, amply successful. Mary felt prosperous as well; she had just signed the organization's annual return, which was being mailed to the IRS that day. She smiled inwardly as she recalled her status as the highest paid employee of the organization. Leaving to meet a member of Congress for lunch, she thought that she could continue to get by on her annual salary of $195,000.

Jack, Betty, Howard, and Mary will never meet. If they did, however, they would have much to talk about, for they have several things in common:

- Each of them is employed by a nonprofit, tax-exempt organization.
- Each of these organizations is an *applicable tax-exempt organization.*
- Each of these individuals is a *disqualified person* with respect to their organization.

- Each of these signings took place on the same day in 1997.
- Each of these organizations is about to be audited by the IRS.

Four audit notices are in the mail, one to each of these nonprofit organization executives. The IRS agents who will soon be interviewing Jack, Howard, and Mary do not have any particular reason for initiating the examination. They will state—truthfully—that their visit is merely for a routine audit. Betty's situation is somewhat different: The agent read about the museum's real estate transaction in the community newspaper. But:

- Jack's feelings of self-esteem are about to darken into depression.
- Betty's admiration for her stepbrother's negotiation skills is about to turn to shame.
- Howard's energy level and standing at the college are about to plummet.
- Mary's success story is about to have a most unhappy ending.

Why? Because each of these four vignettes involves an *excess benefit transaction.*

A few weeks later, Jack Dunlop met in his office with the IRS agent, Ann Thrope, who conducted the audit. Ms. Ann Thrope explained to Jack her findings as to the hospital's operations. Her decision to write a no-change letter, recommending the continuation of the institution's tax exemption, greatly pleased and relieved Jack, who, now relaxed, expected the discussion to close with some social niceties. Jack, however, had misread the situation; his serenity was untimely.

"So, Mr. Dunlop, that concludes my assessment of the hospital's tax status," Agent Thrope was saying. "I thank you and your staff for their cooperation."

"You are certainly welcome, Ms. Thrope," Jack replied with all the courtesy he could muster. He was due on the golf course shortly, and was musing on what he could say to ease her out of his office, when—

"There is one more item that we need to discuss."

"And that is?" Jack replied, with more unease in his voice than he intended.

"The latest Form 990 filed by the hospital shows that your annual salary is $300,000, not to mention your fringe and retirement benefits. Is that still the case?"

"Yes, it is," Jack responded, his thoughts of green fairways dissipating and his discomfort on the rise.

"Mr. Dunlop, I've compared your salary and other elements of compensation with those being paid to the other hospital administrators in the community. I have also taken into account the fact that the hospital's operations have been quite stable over the years, a circumstance you inherited from your predecessor. Now, I realize that she was paid nearly the same amount, but the records reflect you have been with the hospital less than three years. This is your first job. And isn't it true that you were a political science major in college? That what you have learned about hospital administration you obtained while working here?" Agent Thrope's gesture swept grandly across Jack's office.

"Yes," gulped Jack.

"Mr. Dunlop, I have reached the conclusion that you are considerably overpaid. In fact, I believe that someone in your position, under all of the circumstances, ought not to be paid more than $200,000. Therefore, I am writing this up as an excess benefit transaction case for the two years under examination. Do you understand what an 'excess benefit transaction' is?"

Jack's mind was swirling. The "No" he stammered out seemed to only embolden Ms. Thrope, although in fact no such motivation was necessary.

"In this instance, Mr. Dunlop, the hospital has been compensating you at a level that is higher than is warranted. It has been paying you $300,000 a year, when the proper maximum amount is $200,000. These annual payments constitute excess benefit transactions because you are receiving an annual 'excess benefit' of $100,000."

"Ms. Thrope, please. How can you say such a thing?" Jack was starting to recover, as evidenced by his desire to telephone the hospital's lawyer. "I think my salary is most reasonable for what I do, for the responsibilities I have."

"That is, of course, your opinion, Mr. Dunlop," Ms. Thrope stated firmly. "My view is that, although your predecessor was formally trained in hospital administration, you are not. She was earning nearly as much as you after 20 years on the job here. No other hospital in the region is paying as much as you are receiving. And I'm not even certain you are serving in a full-time capacity: Your employment contract allows you one day a week of outside consulting."

Jack started to tell Ms. Thrope that the consulting permission was inserted at his lawyer's insistence but had never been utilized. Recollection of his lawyer stimulated Jack's thinking further: He'd better say no more until he had received some legal advice.

"Ms. Thrope, I don't profess to understand precisely what you are saying. Perhaps you should just leave your documents behind and I'll have them reviewed by the hospital's lawyer."

"I will do that, Mr. Dunlop. However, this matter does not pertain nearly as much to the hospital as it does to you personally. The legal status of the hospital is not involved. I will be assessing taxes that you alone will be liable for."

Jack could only gape at Ms. Thrope.

She continued. "An excess benefit transaction results in a 25 percent tax on the excess benefit amount. That tax must be paid by the disqualified person involved, which in this case is you, Mr. Dunlop. Inasmuch as the excess benefit here is $100,000 per year, the total excess benefit for the years at issue is $200,000. That means that the excess benefit excise tax I must assess for this two-year period is $50,000."

Fifty thousand dollars! Jack was stunned. Agent Thrope couldn't be serious! How could he come up with $50,000? The mortgage, the car payments, the kids' tuition, the balance due on the club's initiation fee, the . . . .

Jack was having trouble connecting with the rest of Ms. Thrope's words.

". . . there is more," she was saying. "The law requires that the excess benefit be repaid to the hospital, Mr. Dunlop. Thus, one of the consequences of this audit is that you must repay the hospital $200,000. And you must do it soon."

Jack was trying to find his breath, his voice. Two hundred thousand dollars! On top of $50,000! That's impossible, he thought. That's crazy. "Ms. Thrope, something's very wrong here," Jack sputtered. "This is insane! I don't happen to have $250,000 lying around!" Anger was seeping in, beginning to replace jabbering.

"Mr. Dunlop. I understand your reaction. Please try to control yourself." Ms. Thrope was standing now. "One more thing. The $50,000 must be sent to the Internal Revenue Service by the date I mail the notice of deficiency, which I will do as soon as I return to my office. The $200,000 must be repaid to the hospital by the same date. If this is not done, Mr. Dunlop, I'm afraid you will also owe the IRS another sum— an additional tax at the rate of 200 percent. That would be an additional $400,000, sir."

Jack now was choking, any composure now lost. "Ms. Thrope, you really must leave now," he stammered.

"Very well, Mr. Dunlop." Agent Thrope crossed Jack's office. As she went through the doorway, she enjoined: "Don't forget that interest and penalties may be added to the figures I gave you. Enjoy the rest of your day."

Jack headed for the golf course, albeit directly to the 19th hole.

CHAPTER ONE

The Law of Intermediate Sanctions

The federal tax law now includes the long-awaited and much-heralded concept of *intermediate sanctions*—an emphasis on the taxation of those who engaged in impermissible private transactions with tax-exempt public charities and social welfare organizations, rather than revocation of the tax exemption of these entities. With this approach, tax sanctions—structured as penalty excise taxes—may be imposed on disqualified persons who improperly benefited from the transactions and on organization managers who participated in any transaction, knowing that it was improper.

This body of law[1] represents the most dramatic and important package of rules concerning exempt charitable organizations since Congress enacted the basic statutory scheme in this field in 1969.[2] Intermediate sanctions have the promise of transforming the private inurement and private benefit doctrines, and are likely to impact the composition and functioning of many boards of directors of nonprofit organizations.

The purpose of this chapter is to provide an objective summary of the law of intermediate sanctions. Subsequent chapters will contain analyses of and commentary on these rules.

EXEMPT ORGANIZATIONS INVOLVED

Intermediate sanctions apply with respect to public charities[3] and tax-exempt social welfare organizations.[4] These entities are termed, for this purpose, *applicable tax-exempt organizations.*[5] They include any organization described in either of these two categories of exempt organizations at any time during the five-year period ending on the date of the transaction.[6]

Public charities include the following:

- Churches, integrated auxiliaries of churches, and associations and conventions of churches;[7]
- Colleges, universities, and schools;[8]
- Hospitals, similar providers of health care, and medical research organizations;[9]
- Foundations supportive of governmentally operated colleges and universities;[10]
- Units of government;[11]
- Publicly supported charitable, educational, religious, scientific, and like organizations;[12] and
- Organizations supportive of public charities.[13]

Tax-exempt social welfare organizations include entities that are civic in nature, assist a community in various ways, or engage in too much advocacy (usually lobbying) than is allowed for charitable organizations.

There are no exemptions from these rules. All public charities and social welfare organizations are applicable tax-exempt organizations.[14]

EXCESS BENEFIT TRANSACTIONS

This tax scheme has as its heart the excess benefit transaction. When one of these transactions has occurred, tax sanctions are to be imposed on the disqualified persons who improperly benefited from the transaction and perhaps on organization managers who participated in the transaction when they knew that it was improper.

An *excess benefit transaction* is any transaction in which an economic benefit is provided by an applicable tax-exempt organization directly or indirectly to or for the use of any disqualified person, if the value of the economic benefit provided by the exempt organization exceeds the value of the consideration (including the performance of services) received for providing the benefit.[15] This type of benefit is known as an *excess benefit*.[16]

An economic benefit may not be treated as consideration for the performance of services unless the organization clearly intended and made the payments as compensation for services.[17] Items of this nature include the payment of personal expenses, transfers to or for the benefit of disqualified persons, and non-fair-market-value transactions benefiting these persons.[18] In determining whether payments or transactions of this nature are in fact forms of compensation, the relevant factors include whether (1) the appropriate decision-making body approved the transfer as compensation in accordance with established procedures and (2) the organization and the recipient reported the transfer (other than in the case of nontaxable fringe benefits) as compensation on relevant returns or other forms.[19]

With the exception of nontaxable fringe benefits[20] and certain other types of nontaxable transfers (such as employer-provided health benefits and contributions to qualified pension plans), an organization is not permitted to demonstrate at the time of an IRS audit that it intended to treat economic benefits provided to a disqualified person as compensation for services merely by claiming that the benefits may be viewed as part of the disqualified person's total compensation package. Rather, the organization is required to provide substantiation that is contemporaneous with the transfer of the economic benefits at issue.[21]

The phraseology *directly or indirectly* means the provision of an economic benefit directly by the organization or indirectly by means of a controlled entity. Thus, an applicable tax-exempt organization cannot avoid involvement in an excess benefit transaction by causing a controlled entity to engage in the transaction.[22]

Also, to an extent to be provided in tax regulations, the term *excess benefit transaction* includes any transaction in which the amount of any economic benefit provided to or for the use of a disqualified person is determined in whole or in part by the revenues of one or more activities of the organization but only if the transaction results in impermissible private inurement.[23] In this context, the excess benefit is the amount of impermissible private inurement.[24]

Thus, excess benefit transactions include (1) transactions in which a disqualified person engages in a non-fair-market-value transaction with an applicable tax-exempt organization or receives unreasonable compensation, and (2) financial arrangements (to an extent to be provided in tax regulations) under which a disqualified person receives payment based on the organization's income in a transaction that violates the private inurement rules. This latter category of arrangement is known as a *revenue-sharing arrangement*. The Department of the Treasury has been instructed to promptly issue guidance providing examples of revenue-sharing arrangements that violate the private inurement prohibition. This guidance will be applicable prospectively.[25]

Under preexisting law, certain revenue-sharing arrangements have been determined by the IRS to not constitute private inurement;[26] it is to continue to be the case that not all revenue-sharing arrangements are improper private inurement. However, the Department of the Treasury and the IRS are not bound by any particular prior rulings in this area.[27]

Existing tax law standards[28] apply in determining reasonableness of compensation and fair market value.[29] In this regard, an individual need not necessarily accept reduced compensation merely because he or she renders services to a tax-exempt, as opposed to a taxable, organization.[30]

There is a rebuttable presumption of reasonableness, with respect to a compensation arrangement with a disqualified person.[31] This presumption arises where the arrangement was approved by a board of directors or trustees (or a committee of the board) that met these criteria:

- Composed entirely of individuals unrelated to and not subject to the control of the disqualified person(s) involved in the arrangement;
- Obtained and relied on appropriate data as to comparability; and
- Adequately documented the basis for its determination.[32]

The first of these criteria essentially requires an *independent* board (as opposed to a *captive* board). A reciprocal approval arrangement does not satisfy the independence requirement. Such an arrangement occurs where an individual approves compensation of a disqualified person and the disqualified person, in turn, approves the individual's compensation.[33]

The appropriate data required in the second criterion include: compensation levels paid by similarly situated organizations, both tax-exempt and taxable, for functionally comparable positions; the location of the organization, taking into account the availability of similar specialties in the geographic area; compensation surveys conducted by nationally recognized independent firms; and written offers from similar institutions competing for the services of the disqualified person.[34]

In the third of these criteria, adequate documentation includes an evaluation of the individual whose compensation was being established, and the basis for determining that the individual's compensation was reasonable in light of that evaluation and data.[35] The fact that a state or local legislative or agency body may have authorized or approved a particular compensation package paid to a disqualified person is not determinative of the reasonableness of the compensation paid.[36]

If these three criteria are satisfied, penalty excise taxes can be imposed only if the IRS develops sufficient contrary evidence to rebut the probative value of the evidence put forth by the parties to the transaction. For example, the IRS could establish that the compensation data relied on by the parties was not for functionally comparable positions, or that the disqualified person in fact did not substantially perform the responsibilities of the position.[37] A similar rebuttable presumption arises with respect to the reasonableness of the valuation of property sold or otherwise transferred (or purchased) by an organization to (or from) a disqualified person if the sale or transfer (or purchase) is approved by an independent board that uses appropriate comparability data and adequately documents its determination. The Department of the Treasury and the IRS have been instructed to issue guidance in connection with the reasonableness standard incorporating this presumption.[38]

DISQUALIFIED PERSONS

For purposes of the sanctions, the term *disqualified person* means:

- Any person who was, at any time during the five-year period ending on the date of the transaction involved, in a position to exercise substantial influence over the affairs of the organization (whether by virtue of being an organization manager or otherwise);[39]
- A member of the family of an individual described in the preceding category;[40] and
- An entity in which individuals described in the preceding two categories own more than 35 percent of an interest.[41]

A person can be in a position to exercise substantial influence over a tax-exempt organization even when that person is not an employee of (and does not receive any compensation directly from) a tax-exempt organization but is formally an employee of (and is directly compensated by) a subsidiary, including a taxable subsidiary, that is controlled by the parent tax-exempt organization.[42]

An individual having the title of *trustee*, *director*, or *officer* does not automatically have the status of disqualified person.[43] Although, in the view of the IRS, all physicians who are on the medical staff of a hospital or similar organization are insiders for purposes of the private inurement proscription,[44] a physician is a disqualified person under the intermediate sanctions rules only if he or she is in a position to exercise substantial influence over the affairs of the organization.[45]

The Department of the Treasury is granted the authority to promulgate rules exempting broad categories of individuals from the category of disqualified persons (such as full-time bona fide employees who receive economic benefits of less than a threshold amount, or individuals who have taken a vow of poverty).[46]

An *organization manager* is a trustee, director, or officer of the applicable tax-exempt organization, as well as an individual having powers or responsibilities similar to those of the trustees, directors, or officers of the organization.[47] Principles similar to those under the law pertaining to private foundations are to be followed in determining who is an organization manager.[48]

The term *member of the family* is defined as being the following:

- Spouses, ancestors, children, grandchildren, great grandchildren, and the spouses of children, grandchildren, and great grandchildren—namely, those individuals so classified under the private foundation rules;[49] and
- The brothers and sisters (whether by the whole or half blood) of the individual, and their spouses.[50]

Thus, compared to its use with regard to private foundations, this term is defined more broadly in the public charity setting.

Entities that are disqualified persons because one or more disqualified persons own more than a 35 percent interest in them are termed *35 percent controlled entities*.[51] They are:

- Corporations in which one or more disqualified persons own more than 35 percent of the total combined voting power;
- Partnerships in which one or more disqualified persons own more than 35 percent of the profits interest; and
- Trusts or estates in which one or more disqualified persons own more than 35 percent of the beneficial interest.

The term *combined voting power* includes voting power represented by holdings of voting stock (actual or constructive) but does not include voting rights held only as a director or trustee.[52]

In general, constructive ownership rules apply for purposes of de-termined 35 percent controlled entities.[53]

TAX STRUCTURE

A disqualified person who benefited from an excess benefit transac-tion is subject to and must pay an initial excise tax equal to 25 percent of the amount of the excess benefit.[54] Again, the excess benefit is the amount by which a transaction differs from fair market value, the amount of compensation exceeding reasonable compensation, or (pur-suant to tax regulations) the amount of impermissible private inure-ment resulting from a transaction based on the organization's gross or net income.[55] (In addition, as noted below, the matter must be rectified by return of the excess benefit to the applicable tax-exempt organization.)

An organization manager who participated in an excess benefit transaction, when he or she knew that it was such a transaction, is sub-ject to and must pay an initial excise tax of 10 percent of the excess ben-efit (up to a maximum amount of tax for a transaction of $10,000[56]), where an initial tax is imposed on a disqualified person.[57] The tax is not imposed where the participation in the transaction was not willful and was due to reasonable cause.[58]

An additional excise tax may be imposed on a disqualified person where an initial tax was imposed and there was no correction of the ex-cess benefit transaction within a specified time period. This time pe-riod is the *taxable period,* or, with respect to an excess benefit transaction, the period beginning with the date on which the transac-tion occurred and ending on the earlier of:

- The date of mailing of a notice of deficiency[59] with respect to the initial tax; or
- The date on which the initial tax is assessed.[60]

When no correction is made within the taxable period, the disquali-fied person would be subject to and must pay a tax equal to 200 percent of the excess benefit involved.[61]

The term *correction* means undoing the excess benefit to the extent possible and taking any additional measures necessary to place the or-ganization in a financial position not worse than that in which it would be if the disqualified person were dealing under the highest fiduciary standards.[62] If more than one organization manager or other disqualified person is liable for an excise tax, then all such persons are jointly and severally liable for the tax.[63]

The IRS has the authority to abate the intermediate sanctions initial excise tax in certain circumstances, principally where a taxable event was due to reasonable cause and not to willful neglect.[64]

RETURNS FOR PAYMENT OF EXCISE TAXES

Under the law in existence prior to the enactment of intermediate sanctions, charitable organizations and other persons liable for certain excise taxes must file returns by which the taxes due are calculated and reported. These taxes are imposed on public charities for excessive lobbying[65] and for political campaign activities,[66] and on private foundations and/or other persons for a wide range of impermissible activities.[67] The return involved is Form 4720.

Disqualified persons and organization managers liable for payment of excise taxes as the result of excess benefit transactions are required to file Form 4720 as the return by which these taxes are paid.[68] In general, returns on Form 4720 for a disqualified person or organization manager liable for an excess benefit transaction tax must be filed on or before the 15th day of the fifth month following the close of that person's tax year.[69]

A Form 4720 for a disqualified person or organization manager liable for the tax on an excess benefit transaction occurring in the person's tax year ending after September 13, 1995,[70] and on or before July 30, 1996, was due on or before December 15, 1996.[71] The 1995 version of Form 4720 was to be used to calculate and report these taxes. Form 4720 will be revised for tax years ending on or after December 31, 1996, to expressly accommodate the intermediate sanctions taxes.

A person filing a 1995 Form 4720[72] should clearly indicate, at the top of the form, that it is for payment of the intermediate sanctions excise taxes. This indication should state: "For payment of § 4958 excise taxes." Form 4720 should be used as follows:

- Part II-A, columns (a), (b), and (h), to report information about the person(s) liable for and the amount of the tax;
- Schedule A, columns (b), (c), (e), and (f), if the transaction was with a disqualified person, using the 25 percent tax rate;
- Schedule A, columns (c), (e), and (g), if the transaction was with an organization manager, using the 10 percent tax rate, to provide other information requested about the transaction.[73]

REIMBURSEMENTS AND INSURANCE

Any reimbursements, by an applicable tax-exempt organization, of excise tax liability are treated as an excess benefit unless they are included in the disqualified person's compensation during the year in which the reimbursement is made.[74] (This rule is consistent with the rule noted above, which states that payments of personal expenses and other benefits to or for the benefit of disqualified persons are treated as compensation only if it is clear that the organization intended and made the payments as compensation for services.) The total compensation package, including the amount of any reimbursement, is subject to the requirement of reasonableness. Similarly, the payment, by an applicable tax-exempt organization, of premiums for an insurance policy providing liability insurance to a disqualified person for excess benefit taxes is an excess benefit transaction unless the premiums are treated as part of the compensation paid to the disqualified person and the total compensation (including premiums) is reasonable.[75]

Because individuals may be both members of and disqualified persons with respect to a nonexclusive applicable tax-exempt organization (for example, a museum or a neighborhood civic organization) and receive certain benefits (for example, free admission or discounted gift shop purchases) in their capacity as members (rather than in their capacity as disqualified persons), the Treasury Department is to provide guidance clarifying that these membership benefits may be excluded from consideration under the private inurement proscription and intermediate sanctions rules.[76]

SCOPE OF THE SANCTIONS

Intermediate sanctions may be imposed by the IRS in lieu of or in addition to revocation of an organization's tax-exempt status.[77] In general, intermediate sanctions are to be the sole sanction imposed in cases where the excess benefit does not rise to a level where it calls into question whether, on the whole, the organization functions as a charitable or social welfare organization.

In practice, the revocation of tax-exempt status, with or without the imposition of these excise taxes, is to occur only when the organization no longer operates as a charitable or social welfare organization, as the case may be.[78] Existing law principles apply in determining whether an organization no longer operates as an exempt organization. For example, in the case of a charitable organization, that would occur in a year, or as of a year, the entity was involved in a transaction constituting a substantial amount of private inurement.

As under preexisting law, a three-year statute of limitations applies, except in the case of fraud.[79] The IRS has the authority to abate an excise tax penalty if it is established that the violation was due to reasonable cause and not due to willful neglect, and the transaction at issue was corrected within the specified taxable period.[80]

REFLECTION IN ANNUAL RETURNS

Applicable tax-exempt organizations are required to disclose on their annual information return—Form 990 or 990-EZ—the amount of the excise tax penalties paid with respect to excess benefit transactions, the nature of the activity, and the parties involved.[81] This requirement is applicable to returns for tax years beginning after July 30, 1996.[82] Accordingly, affected organizations do not have to include information on intermediate sanctions excise taxes or any other information that may be required with respect to excess benefit transactions on their annual returns for tax years beginning before July 31, 1996.[83]

These returns are to be made available for review by any individual during the organization's regular business hours.[84] Also, upon request of an individual, in person or in writing, a copy of the return must generally be provided at no charge other than a reasonable fee for the costs of photocopying and mailing.[85] This latter requirement, however, does not take effect until 60 days after the Department of the Treasury issues regulations on the point.[86]

EFFECTIVE DATES

Intermediate sanctions generally are effective with respect to excess benefit transactions occurring on or after September 14, 1995.[87] The sanctions do not apply to any benefits arising out of a transaction pursuant to a written contract that was binding on that date and continued in force through the time of the transaction, and the terms of which have not materially changed.[88]

However, parties to transactions entered into after September 13, 1995, and before January 1, 1997, are entitled to rely on the above-discussed rebuttable presumption of reasonableness if, within a reasonable period (such as 90 days) after entering into the compensation package, the parties satisfy the criteria that give rise to the presumption. After December 31, 1996, the rebuttable presumption arises only if the criteria are satisfied prior to payment of the compensation (or, to the extent provided by tax regulations, within a reasonable period thereafter).[89]

FUTURE GUIDANCE

The IRS will be issuing guidance providing interpretations of the intermediate sanctions rules (and the related reporting requirements). On September 12, 1996, the IRS invited comments on these rules.[90] The deadline for the submission of comments was December 12, 1996.

NOTES

1. Internal Revenue Code of 1986, as amended, section ("IRC §") 4958, enacted by § 1311(a) of the Taxpayer Bill of Rights 2, P.L. 104-168, 104th Cong., 2d Sess. (1996), 110 Stat. 1452 ("Act"). The text of this legislation, which was signed into law on July 30, 1996, is reproduced as Appendix A.

   The Senate, on July 11, 1996, adopted the legislation as passed by the House of Representatives on April 16, 1996, without change. The House vote was 425–0; the Senate voted by unanimous consent. There is no report of the Senate Finance Committee and no conference report. Thus, the report of the House Committee on Ways and Means, dated March 28, 1996 (H. Rep. 104-506, 104th Cong., 2d Sess. (1996)) ("House Report") constitutes the totality of the legislative history of the intermediate sanctions rules. The appropriate portion of the House Report is reproduced as Appendix D.

   The IRS provided a brief summary of the intermediate sanctions rules in Notice 96-46, 1996-39 I.R.B. 7.

2. Much of the Tax Reform Act of 1969 consists of enactment of law defining public charities and private foundations, and imposing stringent rules of operations concerning these foundations. Much of the motivation for creation of the foundation rules—fear of considerable abuses—is mirrored in the reason for adoption of the intermediate sanctions rules. As is referenced throughout, a considerable portion of the structure of the intermediate sanctions rules is reflective of the private foundation rules in IRC Chapter 42.

3. A *public charity* is an organization that is tax-exempt for federal income tax purposes (IRC § 501(a)) because it is a charitable, educational, scientific, or like organization (that is, is described in IRC § 501(c)(3)); this type of charitable organization is not (by reason of IRC § 509(a)) a private foundation.

The law of public charities is detailed in Chapter 17 of Hopkins, *The Law of Tax-Exempt Organizations* (6th ed., annually supplemented) (New York: John Wiley & Sons, Inc., 1992) (*"Tax-Exempt Organizations"*).

4. A *social welfare organization* is an organization that is tax-exempt for federal income tax purposes (IRC § 501(a)) because it is described in IRC § 501(c)(4).

   The law of social welfare organizations is summarized in Chapter 28 of *Tax-Exempt Organizations.*

5. IRC § 4958(e)(1).

6. IRC § 4958(e)(2).

7. IRC §§ 170(b)(1)(A)(i) and 509(a)(1).

8. IRC §§ 170(b)(1)(A)(ii) and 509(a)(1).

9. IRC §§ 170(b)(1)(A)(iii) and 509(a)(1).

10. IRC §§ 170(b)(1)(A)(iv) and 509(a)(1).

11. IRC §§ 170(b)(1)(A)(v) and 509(a)(1).

12. IRC §§ 170(b)(1)(A)(vi) and 509(a)(1), and IRC § 509(a)(2).

13. IRC § 509(a)(3).

14. Private foundations (see *supra* note 2) are not included in this tax regime because a somewhat similar system—that involving self-dealing rules (IRC § 4941)—is applicable to them. The self-dealing rules are described in Chapter 20 of *Tax-Exempt Organizations.*

15. IRC § 4958(c)(1)(A).

16. IRC § 4958(c)(1)(B).

17. IRC § 4958(c)(1)(A).

18. House Report at 57.

19. These returns or forms include the organization's annual information return filed with the IRS (usually, Form 990), the information return provided by the organization to the recipient (Form W-2 or Form 1099), and the individual's income tax return (Form 1040). House Report at 57.

20. IRC § 132.

21. House Report at 57, note 8.

22. House Report at 56, note 3.

23. IRC § 4958(c)(2).

24. *Id.*

25. House Report at 56.

26. For example, IRS Gen. Couns. Mem. 39674 (Oct. 23, 1987), 38905 (Oct. 6, 1982), and 38283 (Feb. 15, 1980). House Report at 56, note 4. These three pronouncements from the IRS are summarized in Chapter Three.

27. House Report at 56, note 4.

28. This includes those standards established under the law concerning ordinary and necessary business expenses (IRC § 162). House Report at 56.

29. This concept is essentially the same as that stated in the Treasury Regulations ("Reg.") in the private foundation context. Reg. § 53.4941(d)-3(c)(1).
30. House Report at 56, note 5.
31. This rebuttable presumption is not a matter of statute (that is, it is not in the Act); it is provided in the House Report.
32. House Report at 56–57.
33. *Id.* at 57, note 6.
34. *Id.* at 57.
35. *Id.*
36. *Id.*, note 7. Likewise, this type of authorization or approval is not determinative of whether a revenue-sharing arrangement violates the private inurement proscription (see the text accompanied by note 23 *supra*). *Id.*
37. *Id.* at 57.
38. *Id.*
39. IRC § 4958(f)(1)(A).
40. IRC § 4958(f)(1)(B).
41. IRC § 4958(f)(1)(C).
42. House Report at 58, note 10.
43. *Id.* at 58.
44. IRS Gen. Couns. Mem. 39862 (Nov. 21, 1992).
45. House Report at 58, note 12.
46. *Id.* at 58.
47. IRC § 4958(f)(2).
48. House Report at 59, note 13. See Chapter Two, text accompanied by notes 48–53.
49. IRC § 4946(d).
50. IRC § 4958(f)(4).
51. IRC § 4958(f)(3)(A).
52. House Report at 58, note 11. This rule is identical to that in the private foundation context. Reg. § 53.4946-1(a)(5).
53. IRC § 4958(f)(3)(B). See Chapter Two, text accompanied by notes 54–60.
54. IRC § 4958(a)(1).
55. House Report at 58–59. See the text accompanied by *supra* notes 23–25.
56. IRC § 4958(d)(2).
57. IRC § 4958(a)(2).
58. *Id.*
59. IRC § 6212.
60. IRC § 4958(f)(5).
61. IRC § 4958(b).

62. IRC § 4958(f)(6). See Chapter Two, text accompanied by notes 68–69, and Chapter Four, text accompanied by notes 67–75.

63. IRC § 4958(d)(1).

64. IRC § 4962(a).

65. IRC § 4911 or 4912. See Chapter 14, §§ 4 and 9, of *Tax-Exempt Organizations.*

66. IRC § 4955. See Chapter 15, § 7, of *Tax-Exempt Organizations.*

67. IRC §§ 4940–4948. See Part III of *Tax-Exempt Organizations.*

68. Reg. § 53.6011-1(b) (as amended by T.D. 8705).

69. Reg. § 53.6071-1T(f)(1); Prop. Reg. § 53.6071-1(f)(1).

70. See the text accompanied by *infra* note 87.

71. Reg. § 53.6071-1T(f)(2); Prop. Reg. § 53.6071-1(f)(2). This rule was previously announced in IRS Notice 96-46, *supra* note 1.

72. This form is reproduced as Appendix D.

73. IRS Notice 96-46, *supra* note 1.

74. House Report at 58.

75. *Id.*

76. *Id.,* note 9.

77. *Id.* at 59.

78. *Id.,* note 15.

79. IRC § 6501.

80. IRC § 4962. The term *taxable period* is the subject of the text accompanied by note 60 *supra.*

81. IRC § 6033(b)(11) and (12), and (f), as added by Act § 1312(a) and (b).

82. Act § 1312(c).

83. IRS Notice 96-46, *supra* note 1.

84. IRC § 6104(e)(1)(A)(i).

85. IRC § 6104(e)(1)(A)(ii), added by Act § 1313(a)(1). See Chapter Five. This requirement is inapplicable, however, where, in accordance with tax regulations, (1) the organization has made the requested document "widely available" or (2) the IRS determines, upon application by the organization, that the request is part of a harassment campaign and that compliance with the request is not in the public interest. IRC § 6104(e)(3), added by Act § 1313(a)(3).

86. Act § 1313(c); IRS Notice 96-48, 1996-39 I.R.B. 8.

87. Act § 1311(d)(1).

88. Act § 1311(d)(2).

89. House Report at 60.

90. IRS Notice 96-46, *supra* note 1.

CHAPTER TWO

Meaning and Implications of Intermediate Sanctions

There should be no doubt that intermediate sanctions will have a significant impact on the operations of public charities and social welfare organizations, and on persons who are insiders with respect to them.

As noted in the previous chapter, this body of law holds a promise of transforming the private inurement and private benefit doctrines, and can be expected to influence the composition and functioning of many boards of directors of nonprofit entities.

APPLICABLE TAX-EXEMPT ORGANIZATIONS

The reach of intermediate sanctions is confined to tax-exempt public charities and social welfare organizations. Several other categories of exempt organizations, however, have been the subject of criticism because of transactions that are now termed *excess benefit transactions*. Trade and business associations,[1] social clubs,[2] fraternal organizations,[3] and veterans' organizations[4] have been particularly criticized.

In all likelihood, the principles underlying intermediate sanctions will spill over to affect the analysis of private inurement transactions involving other categories of tax-exempt organizations. The organizations themselves will be able to utilize the law of intermediate sanctions as it develops, to assess whether they are engaging in possibly inappropriate transactions. Moreover, many of these other types of exempt organizations have related charitable organizations—often termed foundations—to which intermediate sanctions pertain.

Nothing in the official legislative record indicates why the concept of applicable tax-exempt organization was confined to public charities and social welfare organizations. The focus of these sanctions has been on charitable organizations from the outset, partly because early efforts to initiate these sanctions occurred in the health care setting.[5] Social welfare organizations have attracted the attention of Congress in recent years, because of some instances of aggressive lobbying by them; thus, it is not surprising that they have become a type of applicable tax-exempt organization.[6] Essentially, Congress seems to want to confine the scope of applicable tax-exempt organizations to those entities that have some public purpose. At the same time, as experience with intermediate sanctions grows—or if some scandal involving other types of exempt organizations is revealed—an expansion of the types of organizations caught up in intermediate sanctions would not be a surprise.

CONCEPT OF DISQUALIFIED PERSONS

The intermediate sanctions rules will reshape and refocus the evolution of the federal tax law regarding persons who are disqualified persons—*insiders*, in the parlance of the private inurement rules—with respect to tax-exempt organizations.

In at least one instance, the IRS has overdone the concept by insisting that, for purposes of the private inurement doctrine, a physician is an insider with respect to a charitable hospital simply by virtue of being on the medical staff of the institution.[7] This clear form of overreaching in this area was trimmed when Congress decreed that a physician is a disqualified person only where he or she is in a position to exercise substantial influence over the affairs of the organization.[8]

Conventional wisdom has long held that any individual who is a director or officer of a tax-exempt organization is, for that reason alone, an insider with respect to the organization.[9] However, in the intermediate sanctions context, Congress has instructed the IRS that even someone who is a trustee, director, or officer of a tax-exempt organization is not automatically a disqualified person.[10]

For example, Henry is a real estate broker and one of 40 members of the board of directors of a college. The board decided to sell a large parcel of substantially appreciated real property that it had owned for several years, and sought to save time by having Henry serve as its broker (rather than shop the market for a broker). Henry, pleasantly surprised by this unexpected development, prepared and presented to the college's president a brokerage agreement; making the most of this windfall, Henry charged the college a broker's fee equal to 10 percent of the sales price, although his normal practice, which is common in his community, is to seek a 5 percent fee. The property eventually sold for $50 million; Henry happily collected a $5 million fee.

The intermediate sanctions penalties would apply in this instance if Henry is a disqualified person. This is an excess benefit transaction, with excess benefit of $2.5 million. Although Henry is a director, that role does not automatically make him a disqualified person. He probably is *not* a disqualified person, inasmuch as he is one of 40 directors and does not appear to exercise substantial influence over the board. (He was not involved in the decision to select himself as the real estate broker.) This economic opportunity was fortuitous for him only because the entire board failed to assume responsibility. Thus, intermediate sanctions would likely not be imposed in this instance.[11] (Nonetheless, this is undoubtedly a private inurement transaction, which could cause revocation of the tax-exempt status of the college.[12])

Yet, having somewhat narrowed the prevailing view as to who is a disqualified person, the legislative history also states that a person can be in a position to exercise substantial influence over a tax-exempt organization, even though that person is not an employee of (and does not receive compensation directly from) a tax-exempt organization, but is formally an employee of (and is directly compensated by) a subsidiary—even a for-profit subsidiary—controlled by the parent tax exempt organization.[13] An illustration of the applicability of this rule is in Chapter Four.

Congress has broadened the concept of the disqualified person by including siblings within the bounds of members of a family.[14] It is a measure of the times that, on this point, Congress has made the boundaries as to who is a disqualified person more encompassing for public charities than for private foundations. This is a dramatic shift in outlook and scope in a mere 25 years.

The resculpting of the idea of the insider has probably been most dramatic in the long term (and most subtle in the short term) through creation of the rule that the Department of the Treasury can issue regulations exempting "broad categories" of individuals from being classified as "disqualified persons." The illustrations used are employees who receive economic benefits below a threshold amount, and individuals who have taken a vow of poverty.[15] Whether Congress intended this exemption or not, the rule has forced the IRS to jettison its penurious view that the private inurement doctrine is absolute in scope. With this new rule, there is clearly an insubstantiality or de minimis test underlying the sweep of the private inurement proscription.

PRESUMPTION OF REASONABLENESS

One of the more intriguing aspects of the intermediate sanctions package is the rebuttable presumption of reasonableness that has been made available.[16] This presumption has some flaws. One of the most striking flaws is structural rather than substantive: the presumption is found in the legislative history of the sanctions,[17] not among the statutory rules.

The Department of the Treasury and the IRS can be expected to adhere to this presumption. (If these agencies elect to ignore it for some reason, it may be anticipated that Congress will add it to the statute—and perhaps broaden it in the process.) There is a school of statutory construction—led by Supreme Court Justice Antonin Scalia—that elects to interpret a statute using its own terms, and not by reference to its legislative history. This approach would suppress the existence of the presumption. Overall, however, this use of legislative history is common in the federal tax context and the great likelihood is that the presumption will be reflected in the guidance formulated by Treasury and the IRS.

Another flaw borders on unfairness. The presumption is available only where the board is comprised *entirely* of individuals unrelated to and not subject to the control of the disqualified person(s) involved.[18] The key ingredient in the presumption is reliance on appropriate data to indicate comparability. A reasonable intermediate sanctions scheme would allow the presumption where a board relied on this type of data irrespective of whether some related individuals were on the board. For example, the presumption could have been made available where the board obtained an opinion as to the reasonableness of the transaction from an independent, competent consulting firm—even if a minority of the board were individuals related to the disqualified person.

There is no inherent harm in having related individuals on the board of trustees or board of directors of an applicable tax-exempt organization. Their service is tolerated in the realm of private foundations, even with the tough penalty regime as to self-dealing. The idea of a presumption is valid, but this presumption is going to be difficult to satisfy.

As discussed below, this presumption is likely to have a significant impact on the composition of many boards of directors of applicable tax-exempt organizations, because of the concept (presumably to be amplified in Treasury and IRS guidance) of the *independent* board. On its face, the definition of an independent board is stringent: the board of directors (or trustees) is to be composed entirely of individuals unrelated to and not subject to the control of the disqualified persons involved in the arrangement. The definitions accorded the terms *unrelated* and *control* will be pivotal in framing the reach of this concept. As is so often the case in settings like this, the definition of an independent board will be applied on a case-by-case basis and the scope of it will evolve as circumstances are presented.

The presumption is not just available with respect to an independent board; it is also applicable where the transaction was approved by a "committee thereof." This phraseology means a committee *of* the board of directors (or trustees). Thus, it is not sufficient for a board of directors to select a review committee composed of individuals who, although independent of the disqualified person(s) involved, are not members of that board. For the presumption to be activated, the committee must—among its other required attributes—be composed entirely of board members.

Another difficulty, perhaps not literally a "flaw," with the rebuttable presumption is the assumption as to the availability of "appropriate data as to comparability."[19] These data will be used most frequently when assessing salaries of disqualified persons. It is one thing to evaluate the compensation package of the chief executive officer of a hospital, the president of a college, or the president of a national advocacy group. Ample surveys and studies have researched these levels of compensation. But when assessing the compensation of, say, a television evangelist or a consultant in a narrow field of interest, comparable data may be lean or even nonexistent. What is an independent board supposed to do when it has searched for comparable data but cannot find it? A denial of a presumption of reasonableness appears unfair if a good-faith effort to locate the data has been made by a truly independent board.

The presumption has a positive aspect. Its terms make it clear that, in making comparisons as to salary and the like (presumably, even in the absence of use of the presumption), the facts involving an applicable tax-exempt organization can be compared to facts involving a taxable organization.[20] Thus, for example, in assessing the reasonableness of a compensation package of the chief executive officer of a charitable hospital, one can take into account the compensation paid to a chief executive officer of a proprietary hospital.

The ultimate irony of this rebuttable presumption rests on the fact that, although the sanctions are imposed on disqualified persons, these persons can do little to construct the facts to bring the presumption into play. To avail himself or herself of the protection of the presumption, the disqualified person is dependent solely on the assistance and cooperation of those (board or committee members) over whom he or she, by definition, has no control. By contrast, when tax sanctions are assessed, usually the person involved can take some reasonable steps to avoid the tax. Under this system, when a board of directors fails to pursue comparable data or poorly documents what search it has made, a disqualified person could become taxed through no fault on his or her part.

BOARD COMPOSITION

The boards of directors (or trustees) of tax-exempt organizations range in number from one to over one hundred. There is very little law on this point at the federal level; state law usually requires at least three directors.

Some tax-exempt entities, often charitable ones, have been in existence for decades and, over time, have evolved venerable, community-based boards, often including powerful business leaders and influential academics. These boards, found at many universities and hospitals (as examples), frequently contain 20 to 40 members. Other exempt charitable organizations have these characteristics: they are relatively new, have a single interest focus, and have a very small board. Indeed, the board of directors of this type of organization may well be controlled and dominated by the founder or founders of the entity. A not-infrequent model is the board of three to five persons: the founder, his or her spouse, and some good friends. This is all perfectly understandable. Why should an individual create and grow an organization, only to watch this successful entity be taken over by strangers who remove him or her from a policy-making position in the process? (It has happened too many times.)

As the private inurement doctrine has evolved, many of the court cases where inurement was found entailed organizations that were dominated by one individual—the person accused of participating in the private transaction.[21] Although these governing boards are not prohibited as a matter of law, the courts are building up some presumptions in this area.

For example, it is the view of the U.S. Tax Court that "where the creators [of a charitable organization] control the affairs of the organization, there is an obvious opportunity for abuse, which necessitates an open and candid disclosure of all facts bearing upon the organization, operation, and finances so that the Court can be assured that by granting the claimed exemption it is not sanctioning an abuse of the revenue laws."[22] The court added that, where this disclosure is not made, the "logical inference is that the facts, if disclosed, would show that the taxpayer [organization] fails to meet the requirements" for tax-exempt status.[23]

In another case, the Tax Court found that all of the directors and officers of an organization were related and it could not find the "necessary delineation" between the organization and these individuals acting in their personal and private capacity.[24] Earlier, a court found the fact that a husband and wife were two of three members of an organization's board of directors required a special justification of certain payments by the organization to them.[25] Before that, an appellate court concluded that one individual who had "complete and unfettered control" over an organization had a special burden to explain certain withdrawals from the organization's bank account.[26]

In still another setting, a court considered an organization with three directors: the founder, his wife, and their daughter. These three individuals were among the board membership of five. The small size of the organization was held to be relevant to qualification for tax-exempt status, with the court finding private inurement and private benefit because of the amount of control the founder exercised over the organization's operations and the "blurring of the lines of demarcation between the activities and interests" of the organization.[27] At the same time, this court observed that "[t]his is not to say that an organization of such small dimensions cannot qualify for tax-exempt status."[28]

The IRS has never been fond of charitable organizations with closed boards; yet it is powerless to prohibit them (although attempts to that end, or at least to discourage them, have been made). For example, the involvement of a public charity as a general partner in a limited partnership was sanctioned by the IRS using preexisting criteria[29] but with the IRS inexplicably adding the observation that the exempt organization was governed by an "independent board of directors made up of church and community leaders," in finding an absence of any unwarranted service of private interests.[30] In another instance, concerning a close operating relationship between a charitable organization and a for-profit fund-raising company, where the IRS had raised questions as to private inurement and private benefit, the IRS became satisfied that the organization could retain its tax exemption once its board of directors was enlarged to provide for control by individuals other than its founder (who was also the sole shareholder of the fund-raising company) and her family. The IRS noted that this alteration of board composition "should do much to provide assurance" that the charity will operate "independently" of the company.[31]

By contrast, the IRS found private inurement, including unreasonable compensation, at a tax-exempt hospital; the IRS observed that the salary of the institution's chief executive officer and president was "not determined by an independent compensation committee."[32] By contrast, a reorganization of a hospital system was approved by the IRS, with any private benefit found to be incidental; the IRS emphasized the fact that "there is broad community representation on the boards of directors of the . . . [exempt, charitable] member entities in the system."[33]

Occasionally, the IRS will manage to work into the terms of a closing agreement or private letter ruling some requirement of a broad-based board or rules as to the functions of a board, but this is in the context of a particular case rather than an enforcement of any general legal requirement. For example, the IRS forced a hospital to: concede that its board of trustees lacked adequate awareness of and control over physician recruitment and retention arrangements undertaken by the institution; agree to have the board's executive committee review and approve the principal physician service agreements; adopt a conflict-of-interest policy applicable to the hospital's trustees and officers; and agree to a set of recruitment guidelines requiring board approval of every financial package provided to recruited physicians.[34]

Before intermediate sanctions were enacted, there were only two circumstances in the law pertaining to public charitable organizations where the federal tax law addressed the subject of board composition: (1) the *facts-and-circumstances test*, and (2) the law concerning *supporting organizations*.

The facts-and-circumstances test is part of the rules by which a charitable organization can be considered a publicly supported charity by virtue of the fact that it receives a substantial portion of its support in the form of gifts and grants from the general public.[35] As a general rule, to be publicly supported in this manner, an organization must directly or indirectly receive at least one-third of its support from the public. However, pursuant to the facts-and-circumstances test, the public support ratio can be as low as 10 percent. For the test to apply, however, the charitable organization must have demonstrated compliance with some of a variety of facts and circumstances that indicate interaction between the general public and the operations of the organization. One of these factors is that the governing board of the organization must be reflective of the community.[36]

A supporting organization is a charitable organization that is not a private foundation, usually because it operates to support and benefit one or more public charities.[37] One of the requirements of the supporting organization rules is that a supporting organization may not be controlled by those who are disqualified persons with respect to it.

Thus, the matter of independent and captive boards in the realm of public charities has simmered and festered, existing in an awkward and unresolved state. The fact that these charities may be perceived as being in one of two camps in this regard has not been a major factor in the development of law concerning them.

Intermediate sanctions have the potential to change all of this. The reason: In applying existing tax-law standards when determining reasonableness of compensation, a rebuttable presumption of reasonableness arises where a compensation arrangement with a disqualified person was approved by an independent board (or an independent committee authorized by and of the board) that met the three criteria stated in Chapter One:

- Composed entirely of individuals unrelated to and not subject to the control of the disqualified person(s) involved in the arrangement;

- Obtained and relied on appropriate data as to comparability; and

- Adequately documented the basis for its determination (for example, the record includes an evaluation of the individual whose compensation was being established and the basis for determining that the individual's compensation was reasonable in light of that evaluation and data).[38]

Harshly stated, intermediate sanctions largely are the problem of the individuals involved—the disqualified persons and, sometimes, organization managers as such—rather than the exempt organization. At the same time, these individuals presumably wish to avoid the sanctions and thus would be amply willing (within the bounds of reason) to shape the governance system of the organization to help them achieve that end. The law imposing the responsibilities of a fiduciary on these individuals is in play here. As directors and, to a lesser extent, as officers, these individuals are obligated to marshal and expend the organization's resources in a prudent manner, as if those resources were their own. This law of fiduciary responsibility has a direct bearing on the type of transactions that are encompassed by intermediate sanctions.

For example, a public charitable organization should have some reasonable basis for determining the amount of the compensation of its chief executive officer. Organizations commonly learn about and base this judgment on the compensation levels adopted by comparable organizations. Thus, the second of the three elements supporting the rebuttable presumption may be relatively easy to accomplish, and may well have been in place before the law creating the presumption was enacted.

Likewise, it is common for this determination to be documented; even where documentation has not been the practice, it is relatively easy for an organization to adopt it. This does not mean that the documentation must be explicitly reflected in minutes of the meetings of the board of directors or in some other similar place where this sensitive and personal information would be publicly accessible. It is enough if the documentation is in a secure and private file, perhaps known only to one or two board members. This would support the third component of the presumption, which requires only that there be a "record."

The first element underlying the rebuttable presumption will frequently be posing the true problem. Presumably, few founders of a public charity will be willing to remove themselves from the board of directors of the organization to the end of having a board that is composed entirely of individuals who are not related to or not subject to the control of the founder(s). There is, of course, a greater likelihood that an individual in this circumstance will accede to an independent committee for this purpose (if possible), although even that approach may be problematic. Thus, some public charities, for very sound reasons, will not be able to secure the protection afforded by this presumption. Being thus exposed, the closed-board type of organization may find itself audited in this regard. (The IRS has not announced any formal program of audit of these entities.)

PRECEDENTS: THE PRIVATE FOUNDATION RULES

It is somewhat rare for a statute to be enacted that has its wording based on a preexisting law, to the extent that the interpretation of the new phraseology is informed by the rules that have evolved constituting interpretation of the preexisting language. But that is the case with respect to intermediate sanctions: the structure of the sanctions and much of their terminology are based squarely on the private foundation rules, particularly those pertaining to self-dealing.[39]

Examples of that point are provided in the next sections.[40] In general, the private foundation rules enacted in 1969 represent the first time Congress enacted rules imposing excise taxes on persons who inappropriately interrelate in some fashion with tax-exempt organizations.[41] Intermediate sanctions utilize the same tax structure: initial and additional taxes, also known as first tier taxes[42] and second tier taxes.[43]

By including the intermediate sanctions taxes as first tier taxes, Congress has accorded the IRS the authority to abate the intermediate sanctions initial excise tax in certain instances.[44] This abatement can occur where the IRS is satisfied that:

- A taxable event was due to reasonable cause and not to willful neglect; and
- The event was corrected within the appropriate correction period.[45]

If abatement is granted, the first tier tax (including interest) is not assessed. However, if an assessment has already taken place, it is abated. If the tax has been collected, it is to be credited or refunded as an overpayment.

A lawsuit for refund of an intermediate sanctions tax may be maintained, subject to the usual prerequisites—including those in the private foundation tax setting—for this type of litigation.[46]

The term *taxable event*, used in conjunction with the private foundation and other exempt organization taxes, has been amended to include the intermediate sanctions taxes, for abatement purposes.[47]

ORGANIZATION MANAGERS

An *organization manager* is defined as a trustee, director, or officer of an applicable tax-exempt organization, as well as an individual having powers or responsibilities similar to those of trustees, directors, or officers of the organization.[48] The legislative history of the intermediate sanctions rules states that principles similar to those under the law pertaining to private foundations are to be followed in determining who is an organization manager.[49]

The concept of the organization manager thus includes any employee of an applicable tax-exempt organization who has final authority or responsibility (either officially or effectively) with respect to an act or a failure to act.[50]

An individual is considered an *officer* of an applicable tax-exempt organization if he or she:

- Is specifically so designated under the articles of incorporation, bylaws, or other constitutive document of the organization; or
- Regularly exercises general authority to make administrative or policy decisions on behalf of the organization.[51]

Officers do not include those who have authority merely to recommend particular administrative or policy decisions but not to implement them without approval of a superior, nor independent contractors such as lawyers, accountants, and investment managers and advisers, acting in those capacities.[52]

An organization manager is not necessarily a disqualified person. For example, one who is a director or officer of an applicable tax-exempt organization is not automatically a disqualified person.[53]

CONSTRUCTIVE OWNERSHIP RULES

As discussed earlier, there are three types of 35 percent controlled entities.[54] The constructive ownership rules applicable in determining these entities are similar to comparable rules in the private foundation setting.[55]

In the foundation context, there are two basic constructive ownership rules:

1. In instances involving corporations, indirect stockholdings are taken into account when they would be taken into account under the constructive ownership rules used in ascertaining losses, expenses, and interest with respect to transactions between related taxpayers.[56]

2. In instances involving partnerships or trusts, the ownership of profits or beneficial interests is determined in accordance with the related taxpayers' constructive ownership rules.[57]

Pursuant to the related taxpayers' constructive ownership rules:[58]

- Stock owned, directly or indirectly, by or for a corporation, partnership, estate, or trust is considered as being owned proportionately by or for its shareholders, partners, or beneficiaries.

- An individual is considered as owning the stock owned, directly or indirectly, by or for his or her family. For intermediate sanctions purposes, the definition of *family* is the same as that encompassed by the phrase *member of the family*.[59]

- An individual owning (otherwise than by reason of the previous rule) any stock in a corporation is considered as owning the stock owned, directly or indirectly, by or for his or her partner.

- Stock constructively owned by a person by reason of the first rule above is, for the purpose of applying all these rules, treated as actually owned by that person. Stock constructively owned by an individual by reason of the second or third rules above is not treated as owned by him or her for the purpose of again applying either of those rules in order to make another the constructive owner of the stock.

The private foundation rules state that stockholdings, profit interests, or beneficial interests that have been counted once (whether by reason of actual or constructive ownership) are not to be counted a second time.[60]

EXCESS BENEFIT INVOLVED

The private foundation self-dealing taxes, which are imposed on self-dealers and foundation managers (but not on foundations),[61] are, as noted, an analog to the intermediate sanctions taxes. These taxes are imposed on the *amount involved*. The intermediate sanctions taxes are imposed on the *excess benefit*.[62]

These two concepts are much the same. The amount involved is the greater of the amount of money and the fair market value of other property given or the amount of money and the fair market value of other property received.[63] An excess benefit arises where the value of the economic benefit by the exempt organization exceeds the value of the consideration received by the organization for providing the benefit.[64]

The process of determining the amount of an excess benefit will be the same as that for determining the amount involved. The procedure will be relatively easy where an excess economic benefit is provided directly to a disqualified person. For example, the payment of compensation by a private foundation to a disqualified person is self-dealing where the compensation is excessive.[65] In that instance, the amount involved is the amount of compensation paid (not just the excess portion). In the intermediate sanctions setting, the excess benefit in an instance of the payment of compensation is the element of the compensation that is found to be excessive.

There is very little law in the private foundation context as to the amount involved. The little law there is discussed in Chapter Four.[66]

CONCEPT OF CORRECTION

An excess benefit transaction must be timely corrected in order to avoid imposition of the additional tax. The requisite *correction* occurs when the excess benefit is undone to the extent possible, and when additional measures are taken that are necessary to place the organization in a financial position not worse than that in which it would be if the disqualified person were dealing under the highest fiduciary standards.[67] This basically is a replication of the comparable private foundation rule.[68]

The scant law on this point is discussed in Chapter Four.[69]

THE "KNOWING" STANDARD

As discussed throughout, the intermediate sanctions initial tax can be imposed on both disqualified persons and organization managers.[70] However, there is a major difference in the basis for imposition of these two taxes. The tax on a disqualified person is imposed when an excess benefit transaction occurs, and the tax on an organization manager can be imposed only where (assuming all other criteria are met) the individual knew that the transaction was an excess benefit transaction.[71] Thus, for example, a disqualified person can be taxed on the excess portion of an amount of compensation even though he or she acted in good faith—that is, did not know that his or her compensation package entailed an excess benefit.

There is only one ameliorating factor in this regard for disqualified persons: the abatement rule. The IRS has the authority to abate an intermediate sanctions initial tax where it is shown that the excess benefit arose in a circumstance where it was due to reasonable cause and not to willful neglect, and that the matter was timely corrected.[72] (Theoretically, the initial tax on organization managers is abatable as well, although it is hard to conceive of a situation where an organization manager knew that he or she was participating in an excess benefit transaction, yet had ground to show reasonable cause.)

The distinction between the bases for imposition of these two taxes is also in the private foundation self-dealing rules.[73] There, the term *knowing* means that the individual involved:

- Had actual knowledge of sufficient facts so that, based solely on those facts, the transaction would be an act of self-dealing;
- Was aware that the act, under the circumstances, might violate the federal tax law rules concerning self-dealing; and
- Negligently failed to make reasonable attempts to ascertain whether the transaction was an act of self-dealing, or in fact was aware that it was such an act.[74]

Knowing does not mean "having reason to know." However, evidence tending to show that an individual has reason to know of a particular fact or particular rule is relevant in determining whether he or she had actual knowledge of that fact or rule. Thus, for example, evidence tending to show that an individual has reason to know of sufficient facts so that, based solely on such facts, a transaction would be an act of self-dealing, is relevant in determining whether he or she has actual knowledge of such facts.[75]

In the foundation setting, the term *willful* is defined. There, participation by a foundation manager is deemed willful if it is voluntary, conscious, and intentional. No motive to avoid the restrictions of the law or the incurrence of any tax is necessary to make the participation willful. However, participation by a foundation manager is not willful if he or she does not know that the transaction in which he or she is participating is an act of self-dealing.[76]

Also, in that setting, a foundation manager's participation is considered *due to reasonable cause* if he or she has exercised his or her responsibility on behalf of the foundation with ordinary business care and prudence.[77]

Even the term *participation* is there defined. It includes silence or inaction on the part of a foundation manager where he or she is under a duty to speak or act, as well as any affirmative action by the manager. However, a foundation manager is not considered to have participated in an act of self-dealing where he or she has opposed the act in a manner consistent with the fulfillment of his or her responsibilities to the private foundation.[78]

TREATMENT OF ITEMS AS COMPENSATION

In determining whether an excess benefit transaction has occurred, an economic benefit cannot be treated as consideration for the performance of services unless the organization clearly indicated its intent to so treat that benefit.[79] The legislative history of the intermediate sanctions rules is silent as to the purpose or intent of this restriction.

A private letter ruling from the IRS (predating the effective date of intermediate sanctions) provides a factual basis by which this rule may be evaluated.[80] A private foundation that operated a museum hired an individual as its director. The compensation package that the director accepted included a salary, some fringe benefits, and a below-commercial-interest-rate home mortgage loan. This package was offered to induce the individual to leave former employment; the new location had a higher average cost of housing. Although the salary involved was higher than the one the individual received in the prior position, the overall compensation package was less than that received by the director's predecessor at the museum. The low-rate loan was given an annual value.

The director was considered by the IRS to be a disqualified person because of status as a foundation manager. Although this individual was not a trustee or officer of the foundation, the director had powers similar to those positions and had final authority or responsibility for acts.[81] In general, a loan from a private foundation to a disqualified person is an act of self-dealing.[82]

Thus, the issue arose as to whether the loan, made as part of the compensation package, was exempt from the self-dealing rules on the ground that it constituted compensation for personal services.[83] The IRS ruled that the exemption was not available, so that the making of the loan was self-dealing. The IRS reasoned that the special rule concerning personal compensation does not (with one inapplicable exception) apply to loans. It noted that the regulations under the personal service exception, which contain various exclusions,[84] are silent as to loans.

An act of self-dealing occurs on the first day of each tax year or portion of a year that an extension of credit from a private foundation to a disqualified person goes uncorrected.[85] Thus, in this case, each year that a balance on the loan is outstanding, an act of self-dealing takes place.

However, the organization operating the museum converted to a public charity in the interim. This caused the self-dealing rules to be inapplicable. The loan arrangement was considered part of a reasonable compensation package for these purposes, so the making of the loan was not a private inurement transaction that otherwise could have jeopardized the museum's tax-exempt status.

Thus, this ruling stands as a classic, albeit infrequent, example of a transaction involving a charitable organization that would have been self-dealing (had the rules applied) but not an instance of private inurement. The outcome represented by this ruling would be largely the same where the intermediate sanctions rules apply because, although the museum director would be a disqualified person with respect to an applicable tax-exempt organization, the value of the loan (an economic benefit) was clearly treated by the organization as consideration for the performance of services. However, if that rationale was attached to the value of the loan after the fact (such as during an audit, where imposition of an intermediate sanctions tax was contemplated), that economic benefit might not be treatable as compensation for services rendered for purposes of showing its reasonableness in the context of intermediate sanctions, because the necessary clear intent is absent. (In any event, the making of the loan is not private inurement.)

TAX TREATMENT OF CORRECTIONS

The additional intermediate sanctions tax is assessed where the excess benefit transaction is not timely corrected. This means undoing the transaction.

In an instance of excessive compensation, an undoing of the transaction requires repayment of the excess portion of the compensation (the excess benefit) to the applicable tax-exempt organization. This repayment will almost always occur in a year subsequent to the year in which the excessive compensation was paid. The disqualified person is then required to make the appropriate adjustment as to taxable income on his or her tax return. Other forms of repayments of excess benefits, such as rent or interest, also raise this issue. (The intermediate sanctions taxes are not deductible as business expenses or gifts.)

For example, Mary, the executive director of the advocacy group, received a salary for 1997 in the amount of $195,000. The IRS determined late in 1998 that her salary for 1997 should not have exceeded $135,000. Mary repaid the excess benefit of $60,000 to the advocacy group in 1999.

Repayment of an excess benefit is treated, for tax purposes, under established tax benefit principles.[86] An accountant who reviewed this topic[87] is of the view that the repayment of an excess benefit is governed by the tax rules pertaining to the repayment of money previously included in income under the claim of right doctrine.[88]

If a taxpayer is required to repay an amount of $3,000 or less that had been included in taxable income in a prior year, the amount may be deducted from income in the year it is repaid.[89] If the amount was originally reported as wages or other ordinary income (which would be the case in an instance of excessive compensation paid to a disqualified person), the repayment would be reported (as a negative item) on the individual income tax return for that year.[90]

If the amount to be repaid exceeds $3,000, the procedure to follow in calculating the tax deduction is complex. Basically, taxpayers have the option of taking a deduction for the amount repaid or a credit against their income tax. Here are the steps to be followed in determining which approach will yield the better result:

1. The taxpayer computes his or her tax for the payback year, claiming a deduction for the repaid amount;
2. The taxpayer computes his or her tax for the payback year, without claiming a deduction for the amount repaid. Then:
   a. The taxpayer refigures his or her tax from the earlier year without including in income the amount repaid in the payback year.

b. The tax determined in step a is subtracted from the tax shown on the tax return of the taxpayer for the earlier year.

c. The number obtained in step b is subtracted from the tax for the payback year computed without the deduction.

How a taxpayer treats the repayment on the payback year's tax return is dependent on which answer above results in less tax.

- If the answer in step 1 results in less tax, the taxpayer should deduct the amount repaid on the same form or schedule on which it was previously reported. For example, the amount may have been reported as self-employment income[91] or wages.[92]
- If the answer in step 2 results in less tax, the taxpayer should claim a credit on the tax return.[93]

In Mary's case, the salary she received from the same organization for 1999 was $135,000. However, her taxable income for that year is reduced by the $60,000 repayment of the 1997 excess benefit. This deduction is allowable in 1999 because the receipt of the excess benefit increased Mary's taxable income for 1997.

There can be a situation where there is no deductibility of an excess benefit by a disqualified person. For example, if a disqualified person sold his or her personal automobile to an applicable tax-exempt organization for an amount that was $5,000 in excess of its fair market value, that transaction would have to be corrected by repaying the $5,000 to the organization. However, because that transaction did not give rise to any increased income for the year of the sale, there would not be any adjustment of income tax liability for the year of the repayment.

REPORTING OF EXCISE TAXES

Applicable tax-exempt organizations are required to include in their annual information return the amounts of intermediate sanctions taxes paid by disqualified persons.[94] Moreover, that statute also requires reporting of any "taxes paid by the organization."

This is a curious provision, inasmuch as the intermediate sanctions rules do not impose any taxes on applicable tax-exempt organizations. This language was carried over from previous intermediate sanctions proposals.

Three earlier intermediate sanctions proposals included an "exit tax" on applicable tax-exempt organizations that attempted to terminate

their exempt status subsequent to engaging in an excess benefit transaction.

Under a proposal for intermediate sanctions, advanced in August 1994, that was to have been part of the Uruguay Round of the General Agreement on Tariffs and Trade, the House of Representatives proposed a rule that would have taxed organizations that terminated their exempt status in an effort to help disqualified persons avoid penalty excise taxes.[95]

At a March 16, 1994, hearing before the Subcommittee on Oversight of the House Committee on Ways and Means, the Department of the Treasury presented a proposal for an exit tax as part of an intermediate sanctions package.[96] The Clinton Administration's health delivery reform legislation also contained an exit tax provision.[97]

There are at least two views as to this anomaly. One is that this phraseology is an error, a vestige of the old idea of an exit tax on applicable tax-exempt organizations. Another view—the one supported by some of the committee staff who worked on the legislation—is that the reporting requirement for "taxes paid by the organization" refers to those situations where an excess benefits transaction tax is imposed on a disqualified person and the person is reimbursed by the applicable tax-exempt organization for the tax. In that circumstance, then, the organization effectively has paid the tax.

IMPACT ON PRIVATE INUREMENT DOCTRINE

As the intermediate sanctions rules evolve, the meaning of the term *private inurement* will be refined.[98] For the most part, it may be anticipated that an excess benefit transaction and a private inurement transaction will be the same thing. Indeed, for a revenue-sharing arrangement to be considered an economic benefit transaction, it must be one that results in private inurement.[99]

However, enactment of intermediate sanctions did not bring any revision of the private inurement rule as it applies in the context of charitable organizations. (As noted earlier, the legislation creating intermediate sanctions also contains a provision engrafting the private inurement language onto the statutory rules for tax-exempt social welfare organizations.[100])

Thus, despite its close proximity to the law of intermediate sanctions, the private inurement doctrine technically is autonomous in relation to the sanctions. The extent to which the IRS and/or the courts will interpret and apply the private inurement rules independent from intermediate sanctions is not clear at this time. If it is done to a large extent, it will be because one or more persons involved in the private activity are considered insiders with respect to the organization, without simultaneously being disqualified persons. For example, the IRS may continue to insist that every director and officer of a charitable organization is an insider with respect to that organization, for purposes of application of the private inurement rule, even though not every director and officer of the organization is a disqualified person for purposes of intermediate sanctions.[101] Likewise, the IRS may continue to decree that every physician on the medical staff of a tax-exempt charitable hospital is an insider of the hospital, for private inurement purposes, even though not every physician in that position is a disqualified person for purposes of the sanctions.[102]

This distinction may prove to be more academic than practical, if the IRS follows the admonition that intermediate sanctions are to be the sole sanction to remedy instances of private inurement, absent situations where the inurement is a substantial part of the applicable tax-exempt organization's operations.[103] It is not likely that an applicable tax-exempt organization would be involved in one or more instances of private inurement that are not substantial in scope, where most or all of the transactions were not excess benefit transactions. Were that to happen, however, the private inurement doctrine would preclude tax exemption, or cause revocation of it, although there may not be any excise taxation of disqualified persons.

It is even less likely that there would be private inurement substantial in scope without involving excess benefit transactions. In that instance, the organization's tax-exempt status would be endangered, irrespective of the application of intermediate sanctions.

IMPACT ON PRIVATE BENEFIT DOCTRINE

The enactment of intermediate sanctions may be expected to have a major impact on evolution of the private benefit doctrine. This is particularly the case if, as discussed above, the concept of the excess benefit transaction and private inurement are interpreted and applied so that they are essentially identical, albeit parallel, doctrines.

Intermediate sanctions are triggered only where the person involved in a transaction with an applicable tax-exempt organization is a disqualified person (just as the private inurement doctrine is invoked only where the person involved with a tax-exempt organization is an insider). This leaves a wide range of potential situations where an excess benefit transaction occurs but no disqualified person is involved. That is, there is a private benefit transaction involving an applicable tax-exempt organization, yet the person acquiring the undue benefit does not exercise any form of substantial influence over the organization. This is where the private benefit doctrine may grow in importance, filling the gap caused by the technical requirements of intermediate sanctions.

The most common examples of private benefit transactions involving a party who is not a disqualified person with respect to the exempt organization are: a form of excess compensation paid to an individual who does not exercise substantial influence over the organization, a lending transaction with such an individual, a rental transaction with such an individual, and a sale of assets to such an individual. A private benefit transaction can occur in relation to a person who is not an individual. An illustration of this is payment of fees to an independent fund-raising firm.[104] Other examples along this line could be payments to accounting, investment counseling, law, and management consulting firms.

Greater use of the private benefit rules may be specifically seen in the health care field because the intermediate sanctions rules treat physicians on the medical staff of an exempt hospital as disqualified persons only where they have a substantial influence over the operations of the institution.[105] Presumably, the IRS will want to continue to examine the interaction of a hospital (or other health care institution) with all physicians. For the most part, the private benefit doctrine will be the only means to do this. Examples of transactions involving exempt health care providers and physicians that may be embraced by private benefit considerations and not intermediate sanctions are: provision of recruitment and/or retention incentives, purchase of medical practices, sale of assets, and participation in partnerships and other joint ventures.

IMPACT ON REVOCATIONS

Congress has made it clear that, absent egregious circumstances, intermediate sanctions are intended to be the sole sanction in the case of an excess benefit transaction involving an applicable tax-exempt organization.[106] Thus, revocations are likely to be even fewer than under preexisting law.

This, too, will be a parallel to the experience under the private foundation rules, where the IRS has almost always pursued imposition of the self-dealing taxes rather than revocation of the tax exemption of a private foundation. At the same time, the IRS has not been hesitant to seek both sanctions—taxes on the self-dealer and revocation of exemption—where circumstances warrant that dual approach.[107]

The IRS has made increasing use of the closing agreement as an enforcement mechanism, applied in lieu of revocation of exemption. If this intent of Congress is followed literally by the IRS, it may be anticipated that this use of closing agreements will be lessened. But it is by no means clear that this will be the outcome. It may depend on whether this element of congressional intent is embodied in the tax regulations.[108]

ROLE OF CONFLICT-OF-INTEREST POLICIES

One of the unanticipated consequences of enactment of intermediate sanctions will be the impetus they will provide in stimulating adoption of conflict-of-interest policies by applicable (and other) tax-exempt organizations. Prudent boards of directors, officers, and key staff of exempt organizations will be seeking to avoid excess benefit transactions. There are two principal ways to do this. One way is to avoid transactions with disqualified persons altogether. Another way is to create and maintain contemporaneous and ample records forming a base of evidence demonstrating the reasonableness of transactions. A functioning conflict-of-interest policy can smoke out these potential transactions at the outset. Or, if the transaction is consummated, notwithstanding the involvement of a disqualified person, a conflict-of-interest policy can force the board to face the conflict and accord the details of the proposed transaction a greater degree of scrutiny.

Indeed, not entirely coincidentally, the IRS—faced with loss of its rule that the board of directors of certain health care delivery entities can be comprised of no more than 20 percent of the physicians practicing at the entity[109]—is in the process of allowing physicians on the boards of these charitable entities to an extent of as much as 49 percent.[110] This is to be permitted, however, only where the institution can show that it nonetheless will be operated primarily for charitable purposes. One of the principal ways the IRS expects that showing to be made is by demonstration of an effective conflict-of-interest policy.

In the view of the IRS, a conflict-of-interest policy should have the following elements:

- Disclosure by interested parties of financial interests and all material facts relating to them;
- Procedures for determining whether the financial interest of the interested person may result in a conflict of interest;

- Procedures for addressing an identified conflict of interest;
- Procedures for adequate record keeping;
- Ensuring that the policy is distributed to all trustees, officers, and members of committees with board-delegated powers, and requiring an annual statement from these individuals; and
- Procedures for application of the policy to a compensation committee.[111]

INSURANCE AND INDEMNIFICATION

One of the policies applicable tax-exempt organizations will have to consider in the coming months is whether they will reimburse their disqualified persons for payment of the excise tax penalties. This may entail amendment of articles of organization or bylaws to include appropriate indemnification language. Likewise, these organizations should be considering whether they should insure their disqualified persons against this exposure to penalties, either by purchasing the appropriate insurance for the first time or by adding an intermediate sanctions rider to an existing policy.

There are a number of considerations in this regard. They include additional costs and the propriety (or, depending on the viewpoint, seeming impropriety) of providing this benefit and coverage.

There is a legal problem as well, which centers largely on payment (by direct reimbursement or by insurance) of amounts arising by reason of assessment of second-tier taxes. Inasmuch as this tax rate is 200 percent of an excess benefit,[112] the opportunity is ripe for payment of the penalty, directly or indirectly, to be another excess benefit transaction because the payment of the penalty is regarded as additional compensation.[113] Particularly if the original transgression involved excessive compensation, payment of an additional tax could trigger another round of penalties and a requirement that the second-level excess benefit be returned to the exempt organization, thereby frustrating the point of the reimbursement or coverage.

At a minimum, an exempt organization in this circumstance should write its policy as to reimbursement or coverage so that separate excess benefit transactions are not triggered. This may be done by (1) including a requirement that the reimbursement or coverage will be provided only where it amounts to reasonable compensation (taking into account other compensation)[114] and/or (2) not extending the reimbursement or coverage to the second-tier taxes.

EFFICACY OF RULES

There are those who contend that intermediate sanctions will have little impact because the IRS lacks the resources to enforce these new rules.[115] This is an erroneous conclusion, for at least two reasons:

1. Intermediate sanctions play to the strength of the IRS in this era of downsizing and shrinking governmental budgets. The IRS is forced to more carefully pick and choose its cases, which are then used to set examples. One or two well-publicized cases, which the IRS can easily cause to materialize, are all that is required. The rest of the charitable community quickly gets the point in this setting. A classic case in point—rested on the private inurement doctrine—is the one involving Hermann Hospital and its physician recruitment program.[116] The IRS's use of this hospital as an example, including the publicity surrounding public disclosure of the closing agreement, transformed the physician recruitment and retention practices of hundreds of hospitals throughout the country. It had a much larger impact than dozens of audits.

2. The intermediate sanctions rules were not enacted to provide the IRS with hundreds of cases to process; they are intended to be self-enforcing. The sanctions are designed to have an *in terrorem* effect. For the most part, the sanctions will work just as the private foundation self-dealing rules have: the foundation community has generally brought itself into compliance with the foundation rules, and the charitable community will do the same with intermediate sanctions. A few well-publicized cases will provide any needed additional incentives.

CRITICISMS

The principal criticism of intermediate sanctions is that the overall record of the operations of public charities and social welfare organizations does not warrant the imposition of these penalties. Close to this is a second criticism: the penalties are too severe, entailing as they do rates of tax such as 25 percent and 200 percent. Third, there are those who believe that intermediate sanctions will accord the IRS the opportunity to micromanage the affairs, including the compensation practices, of applicable tax-exempt organizations.[117]

Another criticism revolves around the fact that a disqualified person can become caught up in these penalties—such as by receiving excessive compensation—while acting in a perfectly innocent way. That is, there is no requirement that the disqualified person must know that a transaction is an excess benefit one. Some observers are of the view that, because of the magnitude and sweep of the sanctions and the attendant uncertainty that surrounds them, the *knowing* standard that underlies the tax on organization managers should have been extended to all of the intermediate sanctions taxes. This could have been done as a transitional rule, if not as a permanent rule, to ease in the applicability of these sanctions.[118]

Some criticism attends the rebuttable presumption. This viewpoint sees the presumption as an excellent idea, as far as it goes. Nonetheless, it is considered unfair in the sense that it will be discriminating against organizations that, by their nature and necessity, have a closed board. Much fine work is done by organizations of this nature and, for the most part, the founders and controlling individuals do not abuse the charitable exemption privilege. Because the abuses that occur tend to be in this context, these organizations may receive a significant portion of the IRS's regulatory zeal in this area. It is unrealistic to expect these controlling individuals to relinquish to a group of strangers control over the organization they have fostered and developed, just for the opportunity of utilizing this rebuttable presumption.

There was an answer to this dilemma, but the policymakers summarily rejected it. There are companies and individuals who are expert in evaluating the appropriateness of compensation packages. Assuming the independence of such a consultant from the organization and from the disqualified person whose compensation is under review, it would have been appropriate to extend the rebuttable presumption to cases where the compensation arrangement with the disqualified person was the subject of a timely favorable letter of opinion from a competent executive compensation consultant. This approach would save the intermediate sanctions enforcers considerable time, and would simultaneously enable smaller organizations, which tend to be dominated and controlled by one or two individuals, to retain their existing structure.

The presumption comes close to adopting this approach, in that boards of directors are required to rely on "appropriate data as to comparability," which includes independent compensation surveys by "nationally recognized independent firms."[119] Ideally, there would be a separate presumption of reasonableness, triggered where the board of directors (or trustees) of an applicable tax-exempt organization—irrespective of whether it is independent of the disqualified person(s) involved—relied on a letter of opinion issued to it, as to the reasonableness of compensation, the value of property, or the like, by a "nationally recognized independent firm."

NOTES

1. These associations and other forms of *business leagues* are organizations that are tax-exempt for federal income tax purposes (IRC § 501(a)) because they are described in IRC § 501(c) (6). This category of tax exemption is the subject of Chapter 29 of *Tax-Exempt Organizations.*

   Before 1996 was over, there was discussion by a lawyer on the staff of the Joint Committee on Taxation of the possibility of expanding the concept of the applicable tax-exempt organization to entities described in IRC § 501(c)(6) ("Congress Could Consider Broadening Intermediate Sanctions Law, Aide Says," *Daily Tax Report* (No. 235) G-3 (Dec. 6, 1996)).

2. A *social club* is an organization that is tax-exempt for federal income tax purposes (IRC § 501(a)) because it is described in IRC § 501(c)(7). This category of tax exemption is the subject of Chapter 30 of *Tax-Exempt Organizations.*

3. A *fraternal organization* is an organization that is tax-exempt for federal income tax purposes (IRC § 501(a)) because it is described in IRC § 501(c)(8) or (10). This category of tax exemption is the subject of Chapter 34, § 4, of *Tax-Exempt Organizations.*

4. A *veterans' organization* is an organization that is tax-exempt for federal income tax purposes (IRC § 501(a)) because it is described in IRC § 501(c)(19). This category of tax exemption is the subject of Chapter 34, § 10, of *Tax-Exempt Organizations.*

5. See Appendix C.

6. One of the manifestations of this attention is that § 1311(b) of the Taxpayer Bill of Rights 2 (see Chapter One, note 1) engrafted the private inurement rule onto the criteria for tax-exempt status by reason of IRC § 501(c)(4). The IRS is in the process of issuing guidance as to this rule (Notice 96-47, 1996-39 I.R.B. 8).

7. IRS Gen. Couns. Mem. 39862 (Nov. 21, 1992).

8. House Report at 58, note 12.

9. That is an understandable position, given the principles of fiduciary responsibility. Congress has so legislated in the private foundation setting (see IRC § 4946(a)(1)(B) and (b)(1)).

10. House Report at 58.

11. One observer of intermediate sanctions said: "If you look at the literal language of the new code section [IRC § 4958], and you're a member of a board of 40 people, it could be argued that you're not in a position to exercise substantial influence" ("EO Input on Intermediate Sanctions Wanted, Treasury Official Says," 72 *Tax Notes* 809, 810–811 (Aug. 12, 1996)). If 3 of the 40 board members are also officers and thus have the requisite substantial influence, and the other 37 board members have no other relationship with the applicable tax-exempt organization, does that mean that this 40-person board contains only 3 disqualified persons?

12. See the discussion in Chapter Three, text accompanied by notes 4–12.
13. House Report at 58, note 10.
14. IRC § 4958(f)(4).
15. House Report at 58.
16. See Chapter One, text accompanied by notes 31–38.
17. House Report at 56–57.
18. There are those who hope that the IRS will allow the presumption to operate where there are related or interested individuals on the board of directors who refrained from voting on the transaction at issue. This appears to be an unduly optimistic view.
19. House Report at 57.
20. *Id.*
21. See, in general, Chapter Three.
22. *United Libertarian Fellowship, Inc.* v. *Commissioner*, 65 T.C.M. 2175, 2181 (1993).
23. *Id.* Identical language was used by the court in a prior opinion. See *Bubbling Well Church of Universal Love, Inc.* v. *Commissioner*, 74 T.C. 531, 535 (1980), *aff'd*, 670 F.2d 104 (9th Cir. 1981).
24. *Levy Family Tribe Foundation, Inc.* v. *Commissioner*, 69 T.C. 615, 619 (1978).
25. *Founding Church of Scientology* v. *United States*, 412 F.2d 1197, 1201 (Ct. Cl. 1969), *cert. denied*, 397 U.S. 1009 (1970).
26. *Parker* v. *Commissioner*, 365 F.2d 792, 799 (8th Cir. 1966), *cert. denied*, 385 U.S. 1026 (1967).
27. *Western Catholic Church* v. *Commissioner*, 73 T.C. 196, 213 (1979).
28. *Id.* In *Blake* v. *Commissioner*, 29 T.C.M. 513 (1970), an organization of similar dimensions was ruled to be tax-exempt, although private inurement or private benefit was not at issue in the case.
29. *Tax-Exempt Organizations*, Chapter 46, § 5.
30. Priv. Ltr. Rul. 9438030 (June 28, 1994).
31. Priv. Ltr. Rul. 9417003 (Dec. 1, 1993).
32. Tech. Adv. Mem. 9451001 (Sep. 13, 1994).
33. Priv. Ltr. Rul. 9426040 (April 4, 1994).
34. Closing agreement with Hermann Hospital, dated September 16, 1994, in Bureau of National Affairs *Daily Tax Report* (No. 200), Oct. 19, 1994, at L-1.
35. IRC §§ 170(b)(1)(A)(vi) and 509(a)(1).
36. Reg. § 1.170A-9(e)(3)(v).
37. IRC § 509(a)(3).
38. House Report at 56–57.
39. IRC § 4941. On the eve of enactment of the intermediate sanctions legislation, the director of the Exempt Organizations Division of the IRS,

Marcus Owens, said that the "IRS will be looking to intermediate sanctions to do for public charities what Chapter 42 excise taxes have done for private foundations" ("IRS Has High Hopes for Intermediate Sanctions, Owens Says," 2 *EOTR Weekly* (No. 12) 74 (June 17, 1996)).

40. Another example is the use of the concept of the disqualified person, albeit a somewhat expanded one (see the text accompanied by *supra* notes 7–13).

41. See Appendix C.

42. IRC § 4963(a), as amended by Act § 1311(c)(2).

43. IRC § 4963(b), as amended by Act § 1311(c)(2).

44. The IRS has the authority to abate all but one of the private foundation first tier taxes. The tax that it cannot abate is the one most closely resembling intermediate sanctions: the tax on self-dealing. This is because the self-dealing first tier tax is not a *qualified first tier tax* (IRC § 4962(b)).

    There is a mistake in the statute, which is certain to be rectified by technical corrections legislation. The error stems from the fact that the term *first tier tax* is defined twice in the Internal Revenue Code—and inconsistently. IRC § 4962(b) defines *qualified first tier tax* as "any first tier tax imposed by subchapter A or C of this chapter . . ." (IRC Chapter 42). The difficulty is that the intermediate sanctions tax (IRC § 4958) is lodged in subchapter D of IRC Chapter 42. By contrast, IRC § 4963(a) defines *first tier tax* as including any tax imposed by IRC § 4958(a).

    A lawyer on the staff of the Joint Committee on Taxation said: "The change to present-law Section 4962 was not drafted correctly for some highly technical reasons. The bottom line is that [the] IRS does not have statutory authority to abate [excess benefit transaction] excise taxes, even in cases where an excess benefit was paid to an insider due to a good-faith error." He added that this issue "will be taken care of soon. We consider this a pure technical correction and have already drafted a statutory fix to Section 4962" ("Congress Could Consider Broadening Intermediate Sanctions Law, Aide Says," *Daily Tax Report* (No. 235) G-3, G-4 (Dec. 6, 1996)).

45. IRC § 4962(a). The term *correction period* is defined in IRC § 4963(e). If an intermediate sanctions case is to be filed in the U.S. Tax Court, the period within which the petition must be filed (IRC § 6213(a)) is suspended during the time allowed by the IRS for making any correction (IRC § 6213(e), as amended by Act § 1311(c)(3)).

46. IRC § 7422(g)(2) and (3), as amended by Act § 1311(c)(4).

47. IRC § 4963(c), as amended by Act § 1311(c)(2).

48. IRC § 4958(f)(2). The same rule applies in the private foundation setting (Reg. § 53.4946-1(f)(1)(i)).

49. House Report at 48. The report refers to four specific sections of the tax regulations in this regard; they are referenced in *infra* notes 50–52.

50. Cf. Reg. § 53.4946-1(f)(1)(ii).

51. Cf. Reg. §§ 53.4946-1(f)(2) and 53.4955-1(b)(2)(ii)(B).
52. Cf. Reg. §§ 53.4946-1(f)(2) and 53.4955-1(b)(2)(iii).
53. House Report at 58. Cf. Reg. § 53.4946-1(f)(4). See the text accompanied by *supra* notes 9–10.
54. See Chapter One, text accompanied by note 51.
55. IRC § 4958(f)(3)(B).
56. IRC § 4946(a)(3); Reg. § 53.4946-1(d)(1).
57. IRC § 4946(a)(4); Reg. § 53.4946-1(e)(1).
58. IRC § 267(c).
59. IRC § 4958(f)(4). See Chapter One, text accompanied by notes 49–50.
60. Reg. § 53.4946-1(d)(1)(ii) and (e)(1)(ii).
61. IRC § 4941(a) and (b).
62. IRC § 4958(a) and (b).
63. IRC § 4941(e)(2).
64. IRC § 4958(c)(1)(A).
65. IRC § 4941(d)(1)(D) and (2)(E).
66. See Chapter Four, text accompanied by notes 52–66.
67. IRC § 4958(f)(6).
68. IRC § 4941(e)(3).
69. See Chapter Four, text accompanied by notes 67–75.
70. IRC § 4958(a).
71. IRC § 4958(a)(2).
72. IRC § 4962(a).
73. IRC § 4941(a).
74. Reg. § 53.4941(a)-1(b)(3).
75. *Id.*
76. Reg. § 53.4941(a)-1(b)(4).
77. Reg. § 53.4941(a)-1(b)(5).
78. Reg. § 53.4941(a)-1(b)(2).
79. IRC § 4958(c)(1)(A).
80. Priv. Ltr. Rul. 9530032 (May 3, 1995).
81. See the text accompanied by *supra* note 51.
82. IRC § 4941(d)(1)(B).
83. IRC § 4941(d)(2)(E).
84. Reg. § 53.4941(d)-3(c).
85. Reg. § 53.4941(e)-1(e)(1)(i).
86. During the hearing before the House Subcommittee on Oversight on the Department of the Treasury's initial proposal for intermediate sanctions, on March 16, 1994 (see Appendix C), Leslie B. Samuels, then Assistant Secretary for Tax Policy, said: "Under established tax benefit

principles, repayment of an excess benefit by an insider would be deductible only to the extent that the receipt of the excess benefit increased the insider's income for a prior year."

87. Robert Frank, CPA, Frank & Company, McLean, Virginia.

88. IRC § 1341.

89. IRS Publication 525.

90. Form 1040, Schedule A, line 22, or Form 1040-T, Section B, line o. If the amount was previously reported as a capital gain, it is deducted on Form 1040, Schedule D.

91. If so, it would be deducted on Form 1040, Schedule C.

92. If so, it would be deducted on Form 1040, Schedule A, line 27, or Form 1040-T, Schedule B, line s.

93. Form 1040, line 60 (writing "IRC § 1341" next to the line). A credit cannot be claimed on Form 1040-T.

94. IRC § 6033(b)(11). See Chapter Five, text accompanied by note 17.

95. See Appendix C. This proposal appeared at 11 *Exempt Organization Tax Review* (No. 4) 881 (Apr. 1995).

96. See Appendix C.

97. Health Security Act, H.R. 3600, 103d Cong., 2d Sess. (1994).

98. In general, see Chapter Three.

99. IRC § 4958(c)(2).

100. See the text accompanied by *supra* note 6.

101. See Chapter One, text accompanied by note 43.

102. See Chapter One, text accompanied by note 45.

103. See Chapter One, text accompanied by note 77.

104. A case is pending in the U.S. Tax Court, where one of the issues is whether a charitable organization properly had its tax exemption revoked because of its relationship with a fund-raising company that allegedly was an insider with respect to the charity and engaged in private inurement transactions (*United Cancer Council, Inc.* v. *Commissioner* (Docket No. 2008-91X). This case is discussed in Hopkins, *The Law of Fund-Raising* (2nd ed., New York: John Wiley & Sons, Inc., 1996), Chapter 6, § 15, and Chapter 8, § 12.

105. See Chapter One, text accompanied by notes 44–45.

106. House Report at 59, note 15.

107. E.g., Tech. Adv. Mem. 9627001 (Nov. 10, 1995).

108. Kathleen Nilles, a former tax counsel to the House Committee on Ways and Means, stated: "If that position [intermediate sanctions as nearly the sole penalty] were adopted in regulations, I think we could see a lessening of the closing agreement function. But I'm not sure that the IRS is going to agree that the field is preempted" ("Intermediate Sanctions Move Closer to Reality," 72 *Tax Notes* 397 (July 22, 1996)).

109. This position appears to be based on Rev. Proc. 93-19, 1993-1 C.B. 526. In general, see Chapter 23 (text accompanied by notes 16–18) of Hyatt and Hopkins, *The Law of Tax-Exempt Healthcare Organizations* (New York: John Wiley & Sons, Inc., 1995).

110. This change in policy is reflected in an article included in the IRS's FY 1997 Exempt Organizations Continuing Professional Education Technical Instruction Program Textbook, titled "Community Board and Conflicts of Interest Policy."

111. The elements and workings of a conflict-of-interest policy are discussed in greater detail in Hopkins, *The Legal Answer Book for Nonprofit Organizations* 45–50 (New York: John Wiley & Sons, Inc., 1996).

112. IRC § 4958(b).

113. House Report at 58.

114. Consideration may also be given to the requirement of an agreement with disqualified persons that reimbursements will be timely refunded to the exempt organization to the extent that all or a portion of the reimbursement is considered an excess benefit.

115. E.g., Davis, Jr., and Thomas, "New Penalties Unlikely to Cut Abuse at Charities," VIII *Chronicle of Philanthropy* (No. 21) 52 (Aug. 8, 1996).

116. See the text accompanied by *supra* note 34.

117. E.g., "Former EO Committee Chairs Voice Intermediate Sanctions Concerns," 9 *Exempt Organization Tax Review* (No. 5) 1165 (May 1994).

118. The only solace in this setting is the authority in the IRS to abate these rules (see *supra* note 44).

119. House Report at 57.

CHAPTER THREE

The Sanctions and Private Inurement

The law of intermediate sanctions will, over the coming years, partake heavily of the private inurement doctrine. However, as more time passes, it is likely that the sanctions will have a great bearing on the further development of this doctrine because the resources of the IRS will undoubtedly be invested in application of the standards, rather than application of the private inurement doctrine. Nonetheless, until this shift in emphasis occurs, a complete understanding of the private inurement doctrine is essential to appreciation of the workings of intermediate sanctions.

This interplay of these two bodies of law will occur in two fashions:

1. Concepts of the private inurement doctrine will be used in interpreting the general definition of the term *excess benefit transaction*.[1]
2. More specifically, the law is that an excess benefit transaction includes arrangements where the economic benefit is determined by reference to the revenues of an activity of the organization, where the transaction results in impermissible private inurement under preexisting law.[2]

INTRODUCTION TO PRIVATE INUREMENT

The private inurement doctrine, in addition to being a critical element of the rules enabling organizations to qualify for tax exemption,[3] is the most crucial element in differentiating nonprofit organizations from for-profit ones. The doctrine thus plays a dual role.

The statutory language of the private inurement doctrine requires a tax-exempt organization to be operated so that "no part of . . . [its] net earnings . . . inures to the benefit of any private shareholder or individual."

Nonprofits Defined

United States society is comprised of three sectors. In one sector are the federal, state, and local governments. For-profit entities comprise the business sector. Nonprofit organizations constitute the third sector, which is often referred to as the "independent sector" or the "voluntary sector."

The concept, in the law, of a *nonprofit* organization is best understood through a comparison with a for-profit organization.

In many respects, the characteristics of these two categories of organizations are identical: both require a legal form, have a board of directors and officers, pay compensation, face essentially the same expenses, are able to receive a profit, make investments, and produce goods and services.

However, a for-profit organization has owners—those who hold the equity in the enterprise, such as stockholders of a corporation. The for-profit organization is operated for the benefit of its owners; the profits of the enterprise are passed through to them, perhaps as payment of dividends on shares of stock. This is what is meant by the term *for-profit;* the organization is intended to generate a profit for its owners. The transfer of the profits from the organization to its owners is the inurement of net earnings to the owners.

Like the for-profit organization, a nonprofit organization is able to generate a profit. Unlike the for-profit organization, however, a nonprofit entity generally is not permitted to distribute its profits (net earnings) to those who control and/or financially support it. A nonprofit organization usually does not have any owners (equity holders). Consequently, the private inurement doctrine is the substantive dividing line that differentiates, for law purposes, between nonprofit organizations and for-profit organizations.

General Principles

A nonprofit organization, to be tax-exempt as a charitable, educational, scientific, religious, or like organization, must be organized and operated so that no part of its net earnings inures to the benefit of any private shareholder or individual.[4] This doctrine, known as the *private inurement doctrine,* also applies with respect to other categories of tax-exempt organizations. Where the private inurement doctrine is transgressed, the organization involved may well have its tax exemption revoked.[5]

The concept of private inurement is broad and wide-ranging. Essentially, the doctrine forbids ways of causing the income or assets of a tax-exempt organization (that is subject to the doctrine) to flow away from the organization and to one or more persons who are related to the organization *(insiders),* for nonexempt purposes. The Office of Chief Counsel of the IRS stated the doctrine quite bluntly: "The inurement prohibition serves to prevent anyone in a position to do so from siphoning off any of a charity's income or assets for personal use."[6] Another definition from the same source is that inurement "is likely to arise where the financial benefit represents a transfer of the organization's financial resources to an individual solely by virtue of the individual's relationship with the organization, and without regard to accomplishing exempt purposes."[7]

The essence of this concept is to ensure that a tax-exempt organization is serving a public interest and not a private interest. That is, to be tax-exempt, it is necessary for an organization subject to the doctrine to establish that it is not organized and operated for the benefit of private interests, such as: designated individuals, the creator of the organization or his or her family, shareholders of the organization, persons controlled (directly or indirectly) by such private interests, or any other persons having a personal and private interest in the activities of the organization.[8]

In determining the presence of any proscribed private inurement, the law looks to the ultimate purpose of the organization subject to the doctrine. If its basic purpose is to benefit individuals in their private capacity, then it cannot be tax-exempt even though exempt activities are also performed. Conversely, incidental benefits to private individuals, such as those that are generated by reason of the organization's program activities, will usually not defeat the exemption if the organization otherwise qualifies under the appropriate exemption provision.[9]

The statutory concept of private inurement contemplates a type of transaction between a tax-exempt (usually, charitable) organization and one or more persons (usually, one or more individuals) who have some special, close relationship to the organization. The tax law in this regard has borrowed the term *insider* from the federal securities laws (which prohibit, among other uses of the term, "insider trading") and has applied it to describe persons of this nature. Generally, an insider is a person who, because of a unique relationship with the organization involved, can cause the application of the organization's funds for his or her private purposes by reason of his or her exercise of control of or influence over the organization. In the tax-exempt organization's setting, insiders generally include an organization's founder, directors, trustees, officers, key employees, and members of the families of the foregoing persons.

The IRS invests the definition of the term *insider* with great breadth. For example, the IRS has asserted the view that all physicians on the medical staff of a hospital are insiders in relation to the hospital.[10] In another overly broad reading of the concept, the IRS has staked out the position that all persons performing services for an organization are insiders with respect to that organization.[11]

In the private inurement area, the emphasis of the federal tax law is on "net earnings" and the reference to "private shareholders." The most literal and obvious form of private inurement would be the division of an organization's net earnings among those akin to shareholders, such as members of the board of directors. Rarely does such a blatant form of private inurement occur, although this type of inurement has transpired.[12]

The IRS and the courts have recognized a variety of forms of private inurement. These include:

- Excessive or unreasonable compensation;
- Unreasonable or unfair rental arrangements;
- Unreasonable or unfair lending arrangements;
- Provision of services to persons in their private capacity;
- Certain assumptions of liability;
- Certain sales of assets to insiders;
- Certain participation in partnerships;
- Certain percentage payment arrangements; and
- Various tax avoidance schemes.

The private inurement doctrine does not prohibit transactions between a charitable organization and its insiders. Rather, it requires that these transactions be tested against a standard of *reasonableness*. This standard looks to comparables—that is, how similar organizations, acting prudently, transact their affairs in similar circumstances. Usually, the terms of one or more of these transactions are tested against ordinary commercial practices. An overarching test is whether these transactions were negotiated on an arm's-length basis.

Self-Dealing Prohibitions

Federal tax law contains rules that, in effect, prohibit self-dealing between a private foundation and disqualified persons.[13] Although these rules are confined to charitable organizations that are private foundations, they are in most respects a codification of the private inurement doctrine. In evaluating the potentiality of a private inurement transaction, it is often useful to apply the self-dealing rules to the facts. If a transaction would amount to an act of self-dealing, there is considerable likelihood that it would constitute a form of private inurement.

However, these two sets of rules are by no means parallel, as evidenced by a compensation package made available to the director of a museum, where an element of the package was determined to be self-dealing yet the private inurement doctrine was not transgressed.[14]

Also, these two sets of rules are not mutually exclusive; that is, the self-dealing rules do not preclude revocation of the tax exemption of a private foundation. Thus, if self-dealing is excessive and ongoing, the foundation may well have its tax-exempt status revoked.[15]

The specifics of these self-dealing rules are discussed below, in the context of various forms of self-dealing.

Private Benefit Doctrine

A separate but analogous body of law has been termed the *private benefit doctrine*. This doctrine is a derivative of the operational test (see above) and is potentially applicable with respect to all persons, including those who are not insiders. Thus, it is broader than the private inurement doctrine and, in many respects, subsumes that doctrine. The private benefit doctrine essentially prevents a charitable or like organization from benefiting private interests in any way, other than to an insubstantial extent.[16]

Private Inurement: Is It Absolute?

In the view of the IRS, the private inurement doctrine is an absolute rule of law; that is, there is no toleration of an insubstantial amount of private inurement.[17] The IRS has been quite blunt on the point: "There is no de minimis exception to the inurement prohibition."[18] On this point, the IRS position is often buttressed by the courts. For example, one court stated that "even if the benefit inuring to the members is small, it is impermissible."[19] Another observed that "any inurement, however small the benefit to the individual, is impermissible."[20]

At the same time, the courts frequently engraft some form of insubstantiality threshold onto an ostensibly absolute rule. Thus, one federal court of appeals wrote that "[w]e have grave doubts that the de minimis doctrine, which is so generally applicable, would not apply in this situation"—that is, in the private inurement setting.[21] Indeed, in an illustration of the intermediate sanctions rules influencing the private inurement doctrine, the legislative history underlying the sanctions directs the Department of the Treasury to promulgate rules by which certain incidental benefits received by insiders would not be considered forms of private inurement.[22]

EXCESSIVE COMPENSATION

Excessive or unreasonable compensation is the most common form of private inurement. (Compensation that is reasonable is clearly permissible.[23]) If the individual being compensated is an employee of the organization, *compensation* embraces salaries, wages, bonuses, commissions, fringe benefits, and retirement benefits. Other forms of compensation are payments to vendors, consultants, and other independent contractors (including accountants, fund-raisers, lawyers, and management consultants).

In some instances, an individual will receive compensation from more than one organization, whether or not tax-exempt. A determination as to the reasonableness of this compensation is made by evaluating the aggregate compensation package. For example, in the college and university examination guidelines developed by the IRS, auditing agents are advised that, "[i]f an employee is compensated by several entities, even if the entities have independent boards or representatives, [they are to] examine the total compensation paid to such person by all entities over which the institution has significant control or influence."[24]

This fact is reflected in the annual information return requirements: a tax-exempt organization must list its trustees, directors, officers, and key employees, and the amounts of their compensation (if any).[25] Additional information is required where any of these individuals received aggregate compensation of more than $100,000 from the organization and all related organizations, or if more than $10,000 was provided by one or more of the related organizations.

General Principles

The case law in this area tends to reflect egregious fact circumstances. In one instance, tax exemption for a foundation was denied because those receiving the benefits of its programs were in the employ of the organization's founder.[26] A hospital could not achieve exemption because the physicians who organized the institution obtained certain advantages from its operation.[27] Where the control of an organization was shared by two ministers who were paid unreasonable housing allowances, the tax exemption of the organization was revoked.[28]

Often, other factors also play a role, such as (1) an employee's concurrently receiving other forms of compensation (such as fees or royalties) from or because of the organization, or (2) more than one member of the same family being compensated by the same organization.[29] As an example of (1), royalties and other income flowing to an organization's founder were found to be, in part, the basis for ineligibility for tax exemption.[30] As to (2), in one instance, a college was unable to become tax-exempt because of private inurement; the founder of the college, his two sisters, and two of their spouses comprised the institution's board of trustees.[31] In another of these situations, a foundation failed to obtain tax exemption, in part, because of loans made for the personal benefit of its founder and the members of his family.[32] Similarly, a church could not be tax-exempt because of private inurement; the board of directors of the organization was the founder (its minister), his spouse, and their daughter.[33]

Thus, most of these cases involve circumstances where the compensation of an individual is deemed to be "too high"—unreasonable or excessive. It is possible, however, for items of compensation to be inherently reasonable when viewed in isolation, yet for private inurement to be present inasmuch as the increases in annual compensation were viewed as abrupt and substantial.[34]

Self-Dealing Rules

The payment of compensation (or payment or reimbursement of expenses) by a private foundation to a disqualified person generally constitutes an act of self-dealing.[35] However, the payment of compensation (or payment or reimbursement of expenses) by a private foundation to a disqualified person for the performance of personal services that are reasonable and necessary to carrying out the tax-exempt purpose of the foundation is not self-dealing if the compensation (or payment or reimbursement) is not excessive.[36]

This exception applies without regard to whether the person who receives the compensation (or payment or reimbursement) is an individual.[37] For these purposes, the term *personal services* includes the services of a broker serving as agent for a private foundation,[38] as well as legal, investment counseling, and commercial banking services.[39]

Determining Reasonableness

Whether an item or package of compensation is reasonable is a question of fact. The process for determining reasonable compensation is much like that for appraising a property: it is an evaluation of common factors that have a bearing on its value. That is, it is an exercise of comparing a mix of variables pertaining to the compensation of others. This alchemy is supposed to yield the determination as to whether a particular item of compensation is reasonable or excessive.

Present law is not crystal clear as to the procedure to be used in ascertaining the reasonableness of compensation. Most of what law there is on the point is found in the business expense deduction setting, where compensation must be reasonable to be deductible.[40] The factors to be considered are discussed in Chapter Four.

Whatever the combination of factors that leads to the employment or other retention of an individual—particularly one who is a disqualified person or otherwise an insider—it is important that the information relied on be adequately documented. The documentation might be a record that includes an evaluation of the individual whose compensation was being established and the basis for determining that the compensation was reasonable in light of that evaluation and data.

Revenue-Sharing Arrangements

Revenue-sharing arrangements pose potential private inurement problems because the language of the private inurement doctrine explicitly forbids the distribution of a charitable organization's net earnings.

In one instance, a compensation arrangement based on a percentage of gross receipts was held by a court to constitute private inurement, where there was no upper limit as to total compensation.[41] This opinion suggests that one way to avoid private inurement (or private benefit) when using percentage compensation arrangements is to place a ceiling on the total amount to be paid—assuming, of course, that the total amount is not excessive.

Nonetheless, the court subsequently restricted the reach of this decision by holding that private inurement does not occur when a tax-exempt organization pays its president a commission determined by a percentage of contributions procured by him. The court held that the standard is whether the compensation is reasonable, not the manner in which it is ascertained. Fund-raising commissions that are "directly contingent on success in procuring funds" were held to be an "incentive well suited to the budget of a fledgling organization."[42] In reaching this conclusion, the court reviewed states' charitable solicitation acts governing payments to professional solicitors,[43] which the court characterized as "sanction[ing] such commissions and in many cases endors[ing] percentage commissions higher than" the percentage commission paid by the organization involved in the case.[44]

Thereafter, another court found occasion to observe that "there is nothing insidious or evil about a commission-based compensation system." An arrangement whereby those who successfully procure contributions to a charitable organization are paid a percentage of the value of the gifts received was judged "reasonable," despite the absence of any limit as to an absolute amount of compensation.[45]

The IRS will closely scrutinize compensation programs of tax-exempt organizations that are predicated on an incentive feature by which compensation is a function of revenues received by the organization, is guaranteed, or is otherwise outside the boundaries of conventional compensation arrangements. These programs seem to occur most frequently in the health care context. For example, the IRS concluded that the establishment of incentive compensation plans for the employees of a hospital, with payments determined as a percentage of the excess of revenues over the budgeted level, will not constitute private inurement, where the plans are not devices to distribute profits to principals and are the result of arm's-length bargaining, and do not result in unreasonable compensation.[46] Using similar reasoning, the IRS approved of guaranteed minimum annual salary contracts under which physicians' compensation was subsidized in order to induce them to commence employment at a hospital.[47] The IRS has also explored other forms of productivity incentive programs[48] and contingent compensation plans.[49] Outside the health care setting, for example, the IRS concluded that a package of compensation arrangements for the benefit of sports coaches for schools, colleges, and universities, including deferred compensation plans and payment of life insurance premiums, bonuses, and moving expenses, did not amount to private inurement.[50]

BORROWING ARRANGEMENTS

Although the private inurement doctrine does not prohibit a borrowing arrangement between a tax-exempt organization and an insider, it does impose the requirement that the terms of the arrangement be reasonable. This is particularly the case where the assets of a charitable organization are involved.

General Principles

Where a charitable organization (or other entity subject to the private inurement doctrine) lends money to an insider, all of the rules pertaining to fiduciary responsibility come into play. Because this type of loan is an investment, it should be tested against the standard of prudence. Any placement of funds should be financially advantageous to the organization or at least not disadvantageous to it.

The factors to consider in determining the reasonableness of this type of loan are discussed in Chapter Four. For example, the tax exemption of a school was revoked in part because two of its officers were provided by the school with interest-free, unsecured loans that subjected the school to uncompensated risks for no business purpose.[51]

A court found private inurement as the result of a loan where a nonprofit corporation, formed to take over the operations of a school operated up to that time by a for-profit corporation, required parents of its students to make interest-free loans to the for-profit corporation. Private inurement was detected in the fact that the property to be improved by the loan proceeds would revert to the for-profit corporation after a 15-year term and that the interest-free feature of the loans was an unwarranted benefit to private individuals.[52]

Private inurement was also found in a case involving a tax-exempt hospital and its founder, a physician who operated a clinic located in the hospital building. The hospital and the clinic shared supplies and services, and most of the hospital's patients were also patients of the founding physician and his partner. The hospital made a substantial number of unsecured loans, at below-market interest rates, to a nursing home owned by the physician and to a trust for his children. The court held that there was private inurement to the physician because this use of the hospital's funds reduced his personal financial risk in and lowered the interest costs for the nursing home. The court also found inurement in the fact that the hospital was the principal source of financing for the nursing home, because an equivalent risk incurred for a similar duration could be expected to produce higher earnings elsewhere.[53]

The hospital audit guidelines state that one form of private inurement is inadequately secured loans[54] and that a loan used as a recruiting subsidy is appropriate (assuming the requisite need for the physician in the first instance) as long as the recruitment contract "require[s] full payment (at prevailing interest rates)."[55] These guidelines provide the following factors, which the IRS considers in determining whether a loan made to an insider is reasonable: (1) generally, the loan agreement should specify a reasonable rate of interest (the prime rate of interest plus one or two percent) and provide for adequate security, (2) the decision to make the loan should be reviewed by the board of directors of the tax-exempt organization and should include consideration of the history of payment of prior loans by the insider, and (3) even if determined reasonable, any variance in the terms of the loan from what the borrower could obtain from a typical lending institution must be treated, and appropriately reported, as compensation.[56]

Loans of this nature are likely to be subjected to special scrutiny. One court observed that the "very existence of a private source of loan credit from an organization's earnings may itself amount to inurement of benefit."[57] If a loan, which is reasonable as to its terms, is not repaid on a timely basis, private inurement can occur.[58]

Private inurement can also occur where a tax-exempt organization is borrowing funds from an insider. Essentially, the same criteria are taken into account in evaluating the reasonableness of this type of loan. However, the most important criterion in this context is clearly the rate of interest: an excessive interest rate would be private inurement.

Self-Dealing Rules

The lending of money or other extension of credit between a private foundation and a disqualified person generally constitutes an act of self-dealing.[59] This rule is inapplicable to the lending of money or other extension of credit by a disqualified person to a private foundation if the loan or other extension of credit is without interest or other charge, and the proceeds of the loan are used exclusively for charitable purposes.[60]

RENTAL ARRANGEMENTS

The private inurement doctrine does not prohibit rental arrangements between a tax-exempt organization and an insider. As in other settings, the matter becomes one of determining reasonableness.

General Principles

The factors to be taken into account in determining the reasonableness of a rental arrangement are discussed in Chapter Four. For example, where the applicable tax-exempt organization is renting property from an insider, inflated rental prices are likely to amount to a private benefit inuring to the lessor.[61]

Private inurement can also arise where an insider is renting property from an exempt organization. The principal factor in this context is the amount of the rent payments; below-market rental rates constitute private inurement.

The hospital audit guidelines point out that one form of private inurement is "payment of excessive rent"[62] by an exempt organization and state that areas of concern include "below market leases."[63] The guidelines observe that auditing agents should be alert to the existence of "rent subsidies," noting that "[o]ffice space in the [tax-exempt] hospital/medical office building for use in the physician's private practice generally must be provided at a reasonable rental rate gauged by market data and by actual rental charges to other tenants in the same facility."[64] The guidelines state that it is permissible for a physician to use an exempt organization's facility for both hospital duties and private practice, as long as the "time/use of [the] office . . . [is] apportioned between hospital activities and private practice activities and a reasonable rent . . . [is] charged for the private practice activities."[65]

Self-Dealing Rules

The leasing of property between a private foundation and a disqualified person generally constitutes self-dealing.[66] However, the leasing of property, without charge, by a disqualified person to a private foundation is not an act of self-dealing.[67] A lease is considered to be without charge even though the private foundation pays for janitorial services, utilities, or other maintenance costs, as long as the payment is not made directly or indirectly to a disqualified person.[68]

SALES OF ASSETS

Another application of the private inurement doctrine involves sales of assets of tax-exempt organizations to their insiders.

Basic Principles

An organization may decide to sell some or all of its assets, usually because it no longer wishes to engage in a particular program activity, it is going to cease all present program activities and undertake new ones, or it is going out of business. Sometimes, for a variety of reasons, these assets are sold to one or more insiders with respect to the organization. Transactions of this nature are fraught with the possibilities of private inurement.

A case in point involved a tax-exempt organization that operated a hospital and had research and educational functions, and determined to sell the hospital to gain income for the other functions. Because of the highly specialized nature of the hospital facility, there was a limited market for its sale. Thus, the hospital was sold to a for-profit entity controlled by the members of the institution's board of directors.

The organization went about this process in the proper manner. It secured a valuation from a qualified independent appraiser, and the property was sold at that value ($8.3 million, principally in cash and notes). No loan abatements or other special concessions were offered to the purchasing group. The organization took steps to ensure that it would use arm's-length standards in future dealings with the hospital. A ruling from the IRS was obtained to the effect that the transaction would not adversely affect the tax-exempt status of the organization.

Soon after this sale, the purchasers began receiving inquiries as to resale of the facility. The new organization added beds to the hospital and obtained a certificate of need for additional beds. Less than two years after the sale of the hospital to the insiders, the purchasing organization sold the facility. The resale price was $29.6 million. Each member of the board of the selling organization received in excess of $2.3 million as his or her share of the resale proceeds. The attorney general of the state involved filed a lawsuit, alleging that the sales price was not fair and reasonable. The court agreed, also concluding that the directors acted with a lack of due diligence.

The IRS reviewed this case from a private inurement perspective. The factual issue before the IRS was whether the tax-exempt organization received fair value when it sold the hospital facility. At the state trial, evidence was presented of appraisals using five valuation methodologies; the conclusion was that the value of the assets at the time of sale was approximately $18 million to $21 million. An analysis by the IRS set the value of the facility at $24 million. The IRS concluded that the hospital assets were not sold by the exempt organization for fair market value. This was contravention of the private inurement doctrine; the IRS revoked the tax-exempt status of the organization, effective as of the date of sale of the facility.[69]

In this ruling, the IRS observed: "There is no absolute prohibition against an exempt section 501(c)(3) organization dealing with its founders, members, or officers in conducting its economic affairs." Nonetheless, the IRS was concerned about (in the language of the ruling) a "disproportionate share of the benefits of the exchange" flowing to the insiders. There was nothing inherently improper about the organization's decision to cease the hospital function and to sell the appropriate assets to its directors. However, when the directors resold the hospital facility after a short holding period and experienced a $21.3 million profit, and there was litigation at the state level (with the court finding a breach of fiduciary responsibility), private inurement was found.[70]

Self-Dealing Rules

The sale or exchange of property between a private foundation and a disqualified person generally constitutes an act of self-dealing.[71] This type of self-dealing includes the sale of (1) incidental supplies by a disqualified person to a private foundation, regardless of the amount paid to the disqualified person for the supplies, and (2) stock or other securities by a disqualified person to a private foundation in a bargain sale, regardless of the amount paid for the securities.[72]

An installment sale may be an act of self-dealing either as a sale of property[73] or as an extension of credit.[74]

PRIVATE INUREMENT PER SE

Nearly all instances of private inurement arise where the facts show that the payment—whether it was for compensation for services, rent, interest, or the like—to one or more insiders is not reasonable or is excessive. At the same time, there are forms of private inurement that are such on a per se basis. This means that the structure of the transaction is inherently defective; private inurement is found in the very nature of the transaction. Thus, where the private inurement is of the per se variety, it is irrelevant that the benefit conferred on an insider in some way also furthers the exempt purposes of the tax-exempt (usually, charitable) organization and/or that the amount paid is reasonable.

The most contemporary illustration of private inurement per se is found in the health care setting. For a time, exempt hospitals would engage in the practice of entering into a joint venture with members of their medical staff. A hospital would sell to the venture the gross or net revenue stream expected to be derived from operation of a hospital department or service for a defined period of time. The venture gave advantages to the hospital: it would realize the profits of the program at the outset of the partnership term, and its participation in the venture would help retain the physicians practicing at the institution. The physicians were enamored of the arrangement because they had the incentive (retaining the additional profits) to operate the department or service even more efficiently than might otherwise have been the case.

The IRS came around to the view that hospitals participating in ventures of this nature were jeopardizing their tax exemption, on the ground of private inurement, solely by reason of entering into the transactions.[75] The IRS concluded that hospitals' participation in these ventures did little to accomplish their exempt purposes. The private inurement prohibition was considered violated because "[p]rofit distributions are made to persons having a personal and private interest in the activities of the organization and are made out of the net earnings of the organization."

Private inurement per se thus cannot be defended with the argument that the amounts being paid (in the above instance, to physicians) are reasonable. To date, this doctrine has not been applied with respect to payments that are compensation. The payments to physicians from these revenue-stream joint ventures are considered to be returns on investments. The basis for this differentiation is not clear. However, it probably is a way for the IRS to preserve the viability of a venerable ruling, in which it held that it was permissible for a charitable hospital to pay a hospital-based radiologist a percentage of the adjusted gross revenues from the institution's radiology department in exchange for management and professional services.[76] In finding this arrangement to not be private inurement, the IRS adhered to a reasonable compensation analysis. This precedent may have forced the IRS to make this distinction in the context of its development of the doctrine of private inurement per se.

NOTES

1. IRC § 4958(c)(1)(A).
2. IRC § 4958(c)(2).
3. The private inurement doctrine has been embodied in IRC § 501(c)(3) since the inception of that category of tax exemption (and the federal tax law itself) in 1913. However, the private inurement doctrine was not added to the criteria for tax exemption for social welfare organizations (IRC § 501(c)(4)) until 1996 (by reason of § 1311(b)(1) of the Taxpayer Bill of Rights 2 (see note 6 of Chapter One), creating IRC § 501(c)(4)(B)). This development is the subject of IRS Notice 96-47, 1996-39 I.R.B. 8. The private inurement doctrine is also a part of the rules for tax exemption for labor, agricultural, and horticultural organizations (IRC § 501(c)(5)); business leagues (IRC § 501(c)(6)); social clubs (IRC § 501(c)(7)); cemetery companies (IRC § 501(c)(13)); veterans' organizations (IRC § 501(c)(19)); and state-established organizations providing medical care coverage to high-risk individuals (IRC § 501(c)(26)).
4. IRC § 501(c)(3).
5. The IRS revoked the tax-exempt status of a health care institution on the ground of several instances of private inurement and private benefit (Tech. Adv. Mem. 9451001 (Sep. 13, 1994)); the institution is challenging

this revocation of exemption (*LAC Facilities, Inc.* v. *United States* (No. 94-604T, U.S. Ct. Fed. Cl.).

6. IRS Gen. Couns. Mem. 39862 (Nov. 22, 1991).

7. IRS Gen. Couns. Mem. 38459 (July 31, 1980).

8. Reg. § 1.501(a)-1(c).

9. Reg. § 1.501(c)(3)-1(d)(1)(ii).

10. IRS Gen. Couns. Mem. 39498 (April 24, 1986).

11. IRS Gen. Couns. Mem. 39670 (Oct. 14, 1987).

12. E.g., *Maynard Hospital, Inc.* v. *Commissioner*, 52 T.C. 1006 (1969).

13. IRC § 4941.

14. Priv. Ltr. Rul. 9530032 (May 3, 1995), discussed in Chapter Two, text accompanied by notes 80–84.

15. E.g., Tech. Adv. Mem. 9335001 (April 27, 1993).

16. E.g., *American Campaign Academy* v. *Commissioner*, 92 T.C. 1053 (1989).

17. E.g., IRS Gen. Couns. Mem. 35855 (June 17, 1974).

18. IRS Gen. Couns. Mem. 39862 (Nov. 22, 1991).

19. *McGahen* v. *Commissioner*, 76 T.C. 468, 482 (1981), *aff'd*, 720 F.2d 664 (3d Cir. 1983).

20. *Gookin* v. *United States*, 707 F. Supp. 1156, 1158 (N.D. Cal. 1988).

21. *Carter* v. *United States*, 973 F.2d 1479, 1486, note 5 (9th Cir. 1992).

22. See Chapter One, text accompanied by note 76.

23. One court stated that the "law places no duty on individuals operating charitable organizations to donate their services; they are entitled to reasonable compensation for their efforts" (*World Family Corporation* v. *Commissioner*, 81 T.C. 958, 969 (1983)).

24. *Examination Guidelines for Colleges and Universities*, Internal Revenue Manual, Exempt Organizations Handbook 7(10)(69), § 342.(15)(2), reproduced in Ann. 94-112, 1994-37 I.R.B. 36.

25. Form 990, Part IV.

26. *Horace Heidt Foundation* v. *United States*, 170 F. Supp. 634 (Ct. Cl. 1959).

27. *Harding Hospital, Inc.* v. *United States*, 505 F.2d 1068 (6th Cir. 1974).

28. *Church of the Transfiguring Spirit, Inc.* v. *Commissioner*, 76 T.C. 1 (1981).

29. E.g., *Founding Church of Scientology* v. *United States*, 412 F.2d 1197 (Ct. Cl. 1969), *cert. denied*, 397 U.S. 1009 (1970).

30. *Church of Scientology of California* v. *Commissioner*, 83 T.C. 381 (1984), aff'd, 823 F.2d 1310 (9th Cir. 1987).

31. *Birmingham Business College, Inc.* v. *Commissioner*, 276 F.2d 476 (5th Cir. 1960).

32. *Best Lock Corp.* v. *Commissioner*, 31 T.C. 1217 (1959).

33. *Western Catholic Church* v. *Commissioner*, 73 T.C. 196 (1979), *aff'd*, 631 F.2d 736 (7th Cir. 1980), *cert. denied*, 450 U.S. 981 (1981).

34. *The Incorporated Trustees of the Gospel Worker Society* v. *United States*, 510 F. Supp. 374 (D.D.C. 1981), *aff'd*, 672 F.2d 894 (D.C. Cir. 1981), *cert. denied*, 456 U.S. 944 (1982).

35. IRC § 4941(d)(1)(D); Reg. § 53.4941(d)-2(e).

36. IRC § 4941(d)(2)(E).

37. Reg. § 53.4941(d)-3(c)(1).

38. *Id.*

39. Reg. § 53.4941(d)-3(c)(2). The IRS held that the personal services exception embraces asset management (such as review of and advice regarding asset allocation, including the selection and monitoring of investment managers), coordination of tax matters (such as record-keeping, preparation of returns, and tax planning), other financial services (such as cash management, accounting, accounts payable, financial analysis, and investment appraisals), and administrative assistance in charitable programs (Priv. Ltr. Rul. 9703031 (Oct. 22, 1996)).

40. IRC § 162; Reg. § 1.162-7. E.g., *Kermit Fischer Foundation* v. *Commissioner*, 59 T.C.M. 898 (1990).

41. *People of God Community* v. *Commissioner*, 75 T.C. 127 (1980).

42. *World Family Corporation* v.*Commissioner, supra* note 23, at 970.

43. See Hopkins, *The Law of Fund-Raising* (2d ed., New York: John Wiley & Sons, Inc., 1996), Chapter 4, § 8.

44. *World Family Corporation* v. *Commissioner, supra* note 23, at 970.

45. *National Foundation, Inc.* v. *United States*, 87-2 U.S.T.C. ¶ 9602 (Ct. Cl. 1987).

46. IRS Gen. Couns. Mem. 39674 (Nov. 23, 1987).

47. *Id.*

48. E.g., IRS Gen. Couns. Mem. 36918 (Nov. 11, 1976).

49. E.g., IRS Gen. Couns. Mem. 32453 (Nov. 30, 1962).

50. IRS Gen. Couns. Mem. 39670 (Oct. 14, 1987).

51. *John Marshall Law School* v. *United States*, 81-2 U.S.T.C. ¶ 9514 (Ct. Cl. 1981).

52. *Hancock Academy of Savannah, Inc.* v. *Commissioner*, 69 T.C. 488 (1977).

53. *Lowry Hospital Association* v. *Commissioner*, 66 T.C. 850 (1976).

54. IRS Audit Guidelines for Hospitals, Manual Transmittal 7(10)69-38 for Exempt Organizations Examinations Guidelines Handbook (Mar. 27, 1992), § 333.2(1).

55. *Id.*, § 333.3(4).

56. *Id.*, § 333.3(10).

57. *Founding Church of Scientology* v. *United States, supra* note 29, 412 F.2d at 1202.

58. *Best Lock Corp.* v. *Commissioner, supra* note 32.

59. IRC § 4941(d)(1)(B).

60. IRC § 4941(d)(2)(B).

61. E.g., *Founding Church of Scientology* v. *United States, supra* note 29; *Texas Trade School* v. *Commissioner*, 30 T.C. 642 (1958), *aff'd*, 272 F.2d 168 (5th Cir. 1959).

62. IRS Audit Guidelines for Hospitals, *supra* note 54, § 333.2(1).

63. *Id.*, § 333.3(1).

64. *Id.*, § 333.3(7)(b).

65. *Id.*

66. IRC § 4941(d)(1)(A).

67. IRC § 4941(d)(2)(C). For this rule to be available, the property leased must be used exclusively for charitable purposes.

68. Reg. § 53.4941(d)-2(b)(2).

69. Priv. Ltr. Rul. 9130002 (Mar. 19, 1991).

70. In this case, the appraisals done for the court and the IRS were based on various valuation methodologies; the appraisal relied on by the tax-exempt organization utilized one. In the ruling, the IRS conceded that "no single valuation method is necessarily the best indicator of value in a given case." But, added the IRS, "it would be logical to assume that an appraisal that has considered and applied a variety of approaches in reaching its 'bottom line' is more likely to result in an accurate valuation than an appraisal that focused on a single valuation method." The lesson: sometimes even an independent appraisal and a favorable IRS ruling cannot ward off a finding of private inurement.

    As an example of a current IRS valuation methodology, the IRS published its view as to the principles to follow in valuing medical practices. These principles are in Hyatt and Hopkins, *The Law of Tax-Exempt Healthcare Organizations* (New York: John Wiley & Sons, Inc., 1995), Appendix H (contained in 1997 Cumulative Supplement).

71. IRC § 4941(d)(1)(A).

72. Reg. § 53.4941(d)-2(a)(1).

73. IRC § 4941(d)(1)(A).

74. IRC § 4941(d)(1)(B).

75. IRS Gen. Couns. Mem. 39862 (Nov. 22, 1991).

76. Rev. Rul. 69-383, 1969-2 C.B. 113.

CHAPTER FOUR

Specific Applications of the Sanctions

Intermediate sanctions will have an immense impact on the operations of public charities and social welfare organizations. The essential purpose of the sanctions is to deter certain behaviors. Generation of federal revenues is viewed as an incidental effect.

Much of the law as to what constitutes an excess benefit transaction will rest on rules developed by application of the private inurement doctrine.[1] This chapter focuses on the specific aspects of the practices of public charities and social welfare organizations that are likely to be most affected by the advent of intermediate sanctions.

COMPENSATION

The focus of the intermediate sanctions rules, at least during the opening years, will be on levels of compensation paid to key employees. This has certainly been the emphasis of Congress, fueled in part by the popular media.[2]

As discussed in Chapter Three, the payment of reasonable compensation by public charities and other types of tax-exempt organizations is not private inurement. The law is clear that exempt organizations can have paid employees and can reasonably compensate them without violating the requirements of tax exemption.[3] The same principle of law is applicable with respect to consultants and other independent contractors.

Key employees of public charities and social welfare organizations are disqualified persons because these individuals are situated to exercise substantial influence over the affairs of the organization.[4] Often, these individuals are also organization managers.[5] Excessive compensation paid by an applicable tax-exempt organization is a form of an excess benefit transaction.[6] These fundamental points of the new law are the cornerstone of intermediate sanctions.

The sanctions pose dilemmas for thousands of individuals. They are (or should be) wondering whether their compensation level is too high. Will they be facing hefty excise taxes and a requirement that they disgorge the excess portion of their compensation to their employer?

In the nonprofit mentality, competitive levels of compensation are often shunned—by both employers and employees— because they are perceived as unseemly. However, there is no rule of law that says that a nonprofit employee must be paid a pittance, or that the nonprofit employee's worth in the economic marketplace cannot be equivalent to that of his or her for-profit counterpart. One of the most telling statements in this regard is contained in the report of the House Committee on Ways and Means, which accompanied the intermediate sanctions package.[7] The Committee stated that it intends:

> . . . that an individual need not necessarily accept reduced compensation merely because he or she renders services to a tax-exempt, as opposed to a taxable, organization.[8]

Whether an item of an individual's compensation, or the entire compensation package, is reasonable is a question of fact, not law. The role of law in this regard is to elucidate the elements that the fact finder is to take into account in determining whether compensation is excessive.

The emphasis, in this context, will be on the amount of individuals' salaries. However, the concept of *compensation* is far broader and embraces a wide variety of economic benefits provided, directly or indirectly, to disqualified persons. An analysis of the intermediate sanctions rules includes the following comprehensive (but not exhaustive) inventory of benefits that, separately or collectively, can entail an excess benefit:

- Contributions to pension and profit-sharing plans;
- Forms of deferred compensation;
- Low-interest or no-interest loans;

- Life, liability, and other insurance premiums;
- Personal use of an employer-provided automobile;
- Employer-paid commuting expenses (such as airplane, boat, or train fare);
- Personal use of an employer-provided club membership;
- Personal expenses (such as housing, food and drink, furniture, and legal/tax advice);
- Travel and entertainment expense reimbursements under nonaccountable plans;
- Tuition and related education fees and expenses;
- Vacations (including transportation, food, and lodging);
- Home remodeling;
- Limousines;
- Maid service;
- Health spas;
- Theater/sports tickets and related expenses;
- Bargain purchases or exchanges from an organization by a disqualified person;
- Sales or exchanges in excess of fair market value to an organization by a disqualified person;
- Higher-than-market-rate loans to an organization by a disqualified person; and
- Leases to or from a disqualified person that are favorable to the disqualified person.[9]

The process for determining reasonable compensation is much like that for appraising an item of property: it is an evaluation and application of generally recognized factors that have a bearing on computation of value. It is an exercise of comparing a mix of variables that also pertains to the compensation of others. This alchemy is supposed to yield the determination as to whether a particular item of compensation or a package of compensation is reasonable or excessive.

Present law is not crystal clear about the elements to be taken into account when ascertaining the reasonableness of compensation.[10] Most of what law there is on the point is found in the business expense deduction setting, where compensation must be reasonable to be deductible.[11] (In that setting, an element of compensation that is deemed excessive is cast as a dividend, which is not deductible by the employer corporation.) The legislative history of intermediate sanctions states that "[e]xisting law standards (see sec. 162) apply in determining reasonableness of compensation and fair market value."[12]

The legislative history stresses that "appropriate data as to comparability"[13] are to be assessed. These data include:

- Compensation levels paid by similarly situated organizations, both tax-exempt and taxable, for functionally comparable positions;[14]
- The location of the organization, including the availability of similar specialties in the geographic area; and
- Written offers from similar institutions competing for the services of the individual involved.[15]

The legislative history of intermediate sanctions also includes a rebuttable presumption as to reasonableness of compensation, which itself is a criterion for determining whether compensation is excessive. Thus, another of these elements is whether the compensation package was approved by an independent board of directors (or an independent committee authorized by the board). These bodies are comprised entirely of individuals unrelated to and not subject to the control of the individual whose compensation is under review.[16]

Other criteria include:

- The need of the organization for the services of a particular individual; and
- The amount of time an individual devotes to the position. (An amount of compensation may be reasonable when paid to a full-time employee, yet be unreasonable when the employee is providing services only on a part-time basis.)

As noted earlier, most of the law in this area is found in the context of the business expense deduction. In one of the leading court opinions on the subject, these criteria were enunciated:

- The employee's role in the company, including the employee's position, hours worked, and duties routinely performed, plus any special duties or role;
- Salaries paid to comparable employees in similar companies;
- The character and condition of the company, including its sales, net income, capital value, and general economic fitness;
- Potential conflicts of interest, which could give the employee the ability to disguise dividends as salary, particularly when the

employee is the sole or majority shareholder, and/or where a large percentage of the compensation is paid as a bonus; and

- Consistency of the compensation system throughout the ranks of the company.[17]

No one of these factors is dispositive.[18] The employer's burden of showing that it is entitled to a larger deduction for compensation than allowed by the IRS is particularly heavy when that compensation is paid to a shareholder-officer.[19]

These criteria were applied in a case decided about two months before the intermediate sanctions rules were signed into law.[20] This matter involved an individual who founded a company, owned 95 percent of its stock, and was its president. Although the company had a modest beginning, it became very successful, due largely to the efforts of this individual. His compensation was paid as a salary and bonus. In the first year (1980), his salary was $34,300 and the bonus was $4,000; in the last year reflected in the opinion (1990), his salary was $300,000 and the bonus was $600,000.

The IRS asserted that a portion of the amounts paid to this individual for two years (1989 and 1990) was excessive. His total compensation for 1989 was $766,668; the IRS asserted that $406,666 of that amount was excessive. His total compensation for 1990 was $900,000; the IRS asserted that $495,000 of that amount was excessive. These assertions were sustained by the courts, principally because the compensation scheme was bonus-heavy and salary-light (suggesting masked dividends) and the individual had a conflict of interest (he was the owner of the company and the ultimate decision maker as to his own salary).

The exercise that the IRS and the courts went through in this case is identical to the process the IRS and the courts will be going through in assessing intermediate sanctions with respect to compensation arrangements: determining the criteria to use in ascertaining reasonableness, and then applying the criteria to the particular facts. Just as the IRS endeavors to deny the business expense deduction in the for-profit context (by casting the excess portion of the compensation as a dividend), the IRS will be endeavoring to subject the excessive compensation to excise tax. If this case had involved intermediate sanctions, the liabilities would be significant. This individual would owe, for the two years under audit, a total of $225,417 in initial excise taxes and $901,666 to the tax-exempt organization. If an additional tax was assessed, it would be for $1,803,332![21]

The Prologue profiled the dilemma of Jack Dunlop, a young and influential chief executive officer of a charitable hospital. The compensation committee of the hospital awarded him an annual salary of

$300,000, following his request for that amount, on the rationale that the same salary had been paid to his predecessor. An audit by the IRS covering a two-year period (after September 14, 1995) revealed that the compensation committee had never looked at any salary comparison data before agreeing to Jack's requested compensation, and, unlike his experienced predecessor, this was Jack's first job and his college degree was in political science. His knowledge of hospital management, such as it is, has been derived from what he has learned during his few years on the job.

The IRS agent determined that Jack is a disqualified person with respect to the hospital because he has substantial influence over the affairs of the institution. The agent also concluded that a reasonable salary for the chief executive of a hospital, especially one with Jack's credentials, in the institution's region of the country is $200,000. Thus, the IRS is of the view that the payment of Jack's annual salary is an excess benefit transaction, and the excess benefit (the portion of his salary in excess of the reasonable amount) is $100,000.

Assuming the IRS is correct, Jack is liable for an excise tax equal to 25 percent of the excess benefit he received. This amounts to $25,000 in tax for each year under audit, or a two-year total of $50,000.

In addition, Jack must "undo"—correct—the transaction to the extent possible, which means that, at a minimum, he must repay the hospital $200,000 ($100,000 for each year under audit). If Jack fails to pay this tax and undo the transaction by the close of the taxable period (probably the date the IRS agent, Ms. Ann Thrope, mails the notice of deficiency with respect to the initial tax), he will face an additional tax equal to 200 percent of the excess benefit involved. This tax for the two-year period would be $400,000.

Aside from the matter of interest and certain other amounts (and legal fees), Jack Dunlop could have a total liability in this matter of $650,000—$450,000 in taxes and $200,000 owed to the hospital.

There are no de minimis standards in determining the existence of an excess benefit transaction. (This point is discussed below, in the context of rental transactions.)

REVENUE-SHARING ARRANGEMENTS

The term *excess benefit transaction* includes a transaction in which the amount of an economic benefit provided to or for the use of a disqualified person is determined in whole or in part by the revenues of one or more activities of the organization, but only if the transaction results in impermissible private inurement under preexisting law.[22] The doctrine of private inurement has been applied with respect to a variety of these revenue-sharing arrangements.[23]

The legislative history of this definition of an excess benefit transaction[24] clarifies two points in this regard. First, not all revenue-sharing arrangements amount to improper private inurement and thus not all of them are excess benefit transactions. Second, and more mysterious and troublesome, although the IRS has issued certain pronouncements stating that various revenue-sharing arrangements are not forms of private inurement, the IRS need no longer consider itself bound by these rulings. This is an obvious invitation to the IRS to change its mind in these areas, revoke the pronouncements, and include at least some of these arrangements in its inventory of transactions that entail excess benefit.

The types of revenue-sharing transactions that are specifically referenced in the legislative history of intermediate sanctions are discussed below. Oddly, one of the best known of these types of transactions—the sale, by a department of a hospital, of its net revenue stream to a group of physician insiders—is not mentioned in the legislative history. (The IRS is of the view that these revenue-stream transactions, when they involve sales to insiders, are a form of private inurement that may endanger the tax-exempt status of the exempt organization involved.[25])

As an example, Sally, the valuable director of development at a large publicly supported charitable organization, one evening provided the charity's board of trustees with a report detailing the substantial amount of funds she had raised on behalf of the charity during the past year. Sally made it clear to the board that she had attracted contributions to the charity far in excess of amounts generated by her predecessors. On the spot, she demanded a raise. Specifically, Sally insisted that, in addition to her regular annual salary (which was reasonable under the circumstances), she should receive a commission equal to 10 percent of the gifts received by the charity through her efforts. The board, fearing loss of her services, readily agreed to her demands after desultory discussion.

The very next week, a wealthy individual, who had recently received a direct-mail fund-raising letter written by Sally and sent to all on the charity's donor constituency mailing list, made a $50 million gift to the organization. Sally's next paycheck included a $5 million commission for attracting this gift.

Sally appears to be a disqualified person as to this charity because of her influence in the organization, evidenced in part by the success of her demand for a potentially excessive raise, which triggered essentially no debate. Moreover, the fund-raising activity represented, as to any one contributor, a small amount of effort on Sally's part. This, then, would be an act of private inurement under preexisting law, and thus an excess benefit transaction.

The IRS might agree that Sally was entitled to an additional $50,000 in compensation. This would result in an excess benefit of $4,950,000. The initial intermediate sanctions excise tax would be $1,237,500. Sally would be obligated to also return $4,950,000 to the charitable organization. If Sally cannot correct this transaction within the applicable taxable period, her additional tax bill will be $9,900,000.

Congress has instructed the Department of the Treasury to issue "prompt guidance providing examples of revenue-sharing arrangements that violate the private inurement prohibition; such guidance shall be applicable on a prospective basis."[26]

PROFIT-SHARING PLANS

The legislative history identifies three of these pronouncements that are candidates for review. One of them, issued in 1980, concluded that a charitable organization can, without endangering its tax exemption, maintain a profit-sharing plan for its employees,[27] if the plan is "adequately limited and safeguarded."[28] The case involved a tax-exempt hospital that established and operated a retirement incentive trust and annually made contributions to the trust. The contributions were based on an efficiency improvement percentage applied to the institution's total payroll.

In this determination, the IRS stated that it had come around to the view that a charitable organization can have profits and use some of them to fund a profit-sharing plan for its employees, and not transgress the private inurement rule in the process. For this purpose, the word *profit* means an excess of receipts over expenditures during a given period. The IRS wrote that the "key determination" in this regard is whether an organization's establishment of and contributions to a profit-sharing plan are "done in the proper performance of functions" for which the organization is exempt. It decided that, where the contributions to the plan constitute no more than reasonable compensation, they do not constitute prohibited private inurement.

Indeed, the IRS looked to principles of management theory and concluded that incentive compensation plans, including those that involve various forms of profit sharing, are of material aid in increasing employee productivity, with consequent benefit to the employer. Reference was made to the success of productivity incentive plans formed by nonprofit hospitals as a tool for holding down hospital costs.[29]

Previously, the IRS was of the other view.[30] The conduct of a profit-sharing plan was seen as inherently incompatible with accomplishment of charitable purposes. At issue was the significant potential for conflict between the personal interests of the employees who participate in the plan and the organization's programmatic goals. A profit-sharing plan was viewed as encouraging greater income-producing and profit-making efforts by the employees, and those efforts at maximization of profits, in which the employees would share, could be at the expense of the employer's exempt function.

Indeed, in connection with this change of position, the IRS's lawyers conceded that they "did not give sufficient consideration to the potential for significant benefit to an exempt employer's functions that incentive plans can have." The IRS concluded that benefit to the employees, as long as it constitutes no more than reasonable compensation for services rendered, is not necessarily incompatible or inconsistent with accomplishment of the exempt purposes of the employer but may be merely incidental to those purposes. The IRS's position is now grounded in recognition of this fact and concentrated on devising rules to ensure that the benefit to the exempt function is realized.

Consequently, the current position of the IRS in this regard is as follows: A charitable (and other tax-exempt) organization is permitted to establish and operate an incentive plan that devotes a portion of its receipts to reasonable compensation of productive employees. The IRS's only concern now is whether the plan is properly conceived and administered. In fact, the IRS's lawyers went so far as to say that, in the case of exempt organizations that perform the same function as profit-making entities (such as hospitals), "it seems to make little sense to deny to them sound management practices which may enable them to provide services on a comparable basis." In short, a public charity is allowed to maintain a profit-sharing plan.

Congress has told the IRS that the agency is not bound by its prior rulings in this area. The entire matter of profit-sharing and similar incentive plans for the employees of tax-exempt organizations may therefore be revisited.

Incentive plans are inextricably intertwined with intermediate sanctions, where any of the employees involved are disqualified persons, because the amount of the economic benefit provided to the employees is determined by the revenues of one or more activities of the organization.[31] However, this statute also requires, for the transaction to be an excess benefit one, that the result must be impermissible private inurement under preexisting law. Technically, these plans—as of the time intermediate sanctions were enacted—did not constitute private inurement. Yet Congress has also instructed the IRS to review its position in this area.

The IRS is clearly in a position to go either way on this issue. It is likely that its present view on charity-sponsored profit-sharing plans will not change. However, the IRS completely changed its viewpoint once already. It could do so again.

PERCENTAGE-BASED COMPENSATION

Charitable and other tax-exempt organizations sometimes compensate employees or independent contractors on the basis of, in whole or in part, a percentage of the revenues of the organization. Some fund-raising consultants are paid in this matter. Compensation paid pursuant to these arrangements is, under present law, not a basis for jeopardizing tax-exempt status, as long as that compensation and all other taken together is reasonable.[32]

The IRS had occasion to review one of these compensation arrangements, in a pronouncement that Congress has advised the IRS it may now revisit.[33] This situation involved a contingent compensation agreement between an investment manager and a real estate title-holding corporation,[34] controlled by public charities. The agreement provided that investment management fees are to be calculated as either a percentage of the aggregate purchase price of stock sold or a percentage of the net asset value of the corporation. It was represented that this type of percentage compensation arrangement is customary as a matter of industry practice and necessary to secure competent investment advice.

The private inurement doctrine is inapplicable to the title-holding corporation; it is, of course, applicable to the charitable organizations. The IRS concluded that the agreement did not pose a significant conflict between the personal interests of the investment manager and the interests of the shareholder charities in achieving their exempt purposes. Should such conflicts arise, there are adequate safeguards to protect against operating abuses. Thus, the IRS was of the view that, as long as the compensation was "not unreasonable in magnitude," the charitable organizations would not be in violation of the private inurement proscription.

On this occasion, the IRS observed that the magnitude of (that is, the reasonableness of) compensation is not the sole factor to be considered in ascertaining private inurement. Attention, the IRS said, must also be focused on the "overall interrelationship" between the parties involved. The IRS explained:

Prohibited inurement often exists where a given method of compensation establishes relationships between parties which detract from the exempt purposes of the charitable employer. In this regard, contingent compensation arrangements frequently create a significant conflict between serving the personal interests of employees and maximizing the extent to which ongoing activities may otherwise serve the exempt purposes of a charitable organization. . . . When compensation is determined as a percentage of net earnings, the interests of affected employees may be enhanced by an increase in net earnings through the manipulation of receipts and expenditures (e.g., by an increase in the price or a reduction in the cost of the goods or services provided by the charitable organization) while possibly diverting from the effective achievement of the charitable organization's exempt purposes (e.g., by a reduction in either the number of potential charitable beneficiaries or the quality of the goods or services provided by the charitable organization).

Yet, the IRS said, a percentage compensation arrangement based on net earnings is not per se improper.

The IRS conceded that this fact situation presented private inurement issues because the investment adviser's compensation was dependent on the total number of stocks sold and, subsequently, on the fluctuating value of the title-holding company's property holdings. At the same time, the IRS found that the potential for substantial conflicts of interest was low because the adviser was to be contracted with directly by the title-holding company rather than by its parent charitable organizations. Thus, in achieving their exempt purposes, the parent organizations will be only indirectly dependent on the performance of the adviser.

Moreover, the IRS was able to further distinguish this compensation arrangement from compensation formulas found inherently incompatible with the activities of charitable organizations. The adviser's monthly compensation will be calculated as either a percentage of the aggregate purchase price of shares sold or a percentage of the value of net assets to which the title-holding company holds title, and will not be directly conditioned on any combination of the receipts and expenditures of the title-holding company or its charitable parents. Thus, the IRS concluded, an "incentive to manipulate receipts and expenditures will be lacking."

In another case, a tax-exempt social welfare organization, operating as a prepaid medical service provider, furnished medical services to subscribers by entering into contractual arrangements for medical services with independent groups of private physicians. Under the terms of the contractual arrangements, these medical groups would be compensated by a fixed monthly fee per medical plan subscriber, plus a percentage of certain of the organization's net revenue.

The IRS approved this percentage compensation arrangement.[35] The following factors determined this outcome:

- An arm's-length contractual relationship existed, with the service provider having no participation in the management or control of the organization;

- The contingent payments served a real and discernible business purpose of the tax-exempt organization, independent of any purpose to operate the organization for the direct or indirect benefit of the service provider (for example, achieving maximum efficiency and economy in operations by shifting away the principal risk of operating cost to the service provider so as to alleviate the organization's need to carry large insurance-type reserves);

- The amount of compensation was not dependent principally on incoming revenue of the exempt organization but rather on the accomplishment of the objectives of the compensatory contract (for example, the success of the employer organization and the service provider in keeping actual expenses within the limits of the projected expenses, on which the ultimate prices of charitable services were based);

- Review of the actual operating results revealed no evidence of abuse or unwarranted benefits (for example, prices and operating costs compared favorably with those of other similar organizations); and

- A ceiling or reasonable maximum was established, to avoid the possibility of a windfall benefit to the service provider based on factors bearing no direct relationship to the level of service provided.

Nonetheless, the IRS is of the view that contingent compensation arrangements between health maintenance organizations and private medical service providers provide an opportunity for "abuse and subterfuge."[36] Thus, it has a policy against tax exemption in these cases unless there is a showing of safeguards against operating abuses. At the same time, several contingent compensation plans that satisfied different combinations of these factors have been determined by the IRS to protect against conflicts of interest in a manner that avoids prospects of private inurement.[37]

Today, the IRS is of the view that benefits derived from incentive compensation plans "generally accrue not only to employees, but also to charitable employers (e.g., increased productivity, cost stability) in aiding rather than detracting from the accomplishment of their exempt purposes."[38] But, again, Congress has advised the IRS that it should revisit this subject.

BORROWING ARRANGEMENTS

The focus of the intermediate sanctions rules will, at least initially, be on compensation arrangements, but enforcement activity will by no means be confined to those arrangements. Another area of focus will be borrowing transactions, and the IRS will be looking for the following situations:

- An applicable tax-exempt organization is borrowing money from a disqualified person under circumstances where one or more aspects of the transaction are unreasonable (e.g., the rate of interest is excessive); or
- A disqualified person is borrowing money from an applicable tax-exempt organization under circumstances where one or more aspects of the transaction are unreasonable (e.g., the rate of interest is below market).

The factors to be considered in determining the reasonableness of this type of loan include the following:

- The amount being borrowed—both the amount itself and (particularly where the organization is the lender) its proportionate relationship to the total amount of the organization's investment assets;
- The rate of interest to be paid;
- The duration of the loan;
- The extent to which the loan is secured or unsecured;
- The creditworthiness (past credit record) of the borrower; or
- The approval of the loan by an independent board of directors (or an independent committee authorized by the board).

RENTAL ARRANGEMENTS

Another field of inquiry in this context will be rental transactions. The IRS will be looking for the following situations:

- An applicable tax-exempt organization is renting property from a disqualified person under circumstances where one or more aspects of the transaction are unreasonable (e.g., the rental rate is excessive); or

- A disqualified person is renting property from an applicable tax-exempt organization under circumstances where one or more aspects of the transaction are unreasonable (e.g., the rental rate is below market).

The factors to be taken into account in determining the reasonableness of a rental arrangement, where the applicable tax-exempt organization is renting property from a disqualified person, include:

- The amount and frequency of the rent payments;
- The duration of the lease; or
- The use the tax-exempt organization makes of the rental property.

In the Prologue, a transaction involving a rental arrangement with a tax-exempt museum was previewed. Betty McGowan is director of one of her region's largest museums. Being very influential at the institution, she was able to persuade the museum's board to rent from a partnership (in a transaction after September 14, 1995) the land on which the museum's newest display building now stood.

The partners consist of Betty, her husband, her stepbrother, and her stepbrother's wife. Each of these partners owns an equal-profit interest in the partnership. The museum's board of directors agreed to pay the landlord/partnership $700,000 in rent, as the landlord had demanded. The board did not make any effort to determine the true fair rental value of the property.

IRS agent Ms. Ann Thrope audited the museum, and concluded—utilizing the above criteria—that the annual fair market rental value of the property is $500,000. Agent Thrope also determined that Betty is a disqualified person with respect to the museum because she has substantial influence over the institution's affairs. The lease for the property is with the partnership, however, so the next issue was whether the partnership is a disqualified person with respect to the museum.

A partnership is a disqualified person with respect to an applicable tax-exempt organization if a disqualified person or a member of the family of a disqualified person owns more than a 35 percent profits interest in the partnership. Betty, a disqualified person, owns 25 percent of the partnership. However, her husband, stepbrother, and stepbrother's wife are also disqualified persons because they are members of Betty's family. Thus, 100 percent of the profits interest of the partnership is owned by disqualified persons, which makes the partnership a disqualified person.

Consequently, the lease between the museum and the partnership embodies an excess benefit transaction. The partnership (through its four partners) will be responsible for paying a 25 percent excise tax ($50,000 per year) on the excess annual benefit of $200,000. Moreover, the partnership must return to the museum $400,000 as correction of the excess benefit transaction. If the partnership does not pay the initial tax and undo the transaction in a timely manner (by the end of the taxable period), it will face an additional tax equal to 200 percent of the excess benefit involved. This tax would be $400,000 for each year, or a total of $800,000 for the audit period.

Aside from the matter of interest and certain other amounts (and legal fees), this partnership could have a total liability of $1,300,000— $900,000 in taxes and $400,000 owed to the museum.

As noted earlier, in the context of the discussion of compensation as an excess benefit, there is no de minimis standard underlying the intermediate sanctions penalties. However, actual practice may prove to be otherwise.

As an example, Sam, an influential director on the board of a public charity, sold a parcel of land to the charitable organization for $100,000. Thereafter, an IRS audit brought the determination that the fair market value of the property at the time of sale was no more than $95,000. Assuming that this valuation is accurate, would an intermediate sanctions initial excise tax be appropriate?

A reading of the statutory scheme leads to a conclusion that Sam would owe a penalty tax of $1,250 and must return $5,000 to the public charity. However, the IRS may exercise some discretion here. For example, it has been reported that IRS officials have stated that they would not penalize "minor" excess benefit transactions and that an excess benefit not in excess of 10 percent would not be sufficiently egregious to pursue. According to this report, excess benefits entailing 25 percent or more will be of interest, as will transactions where the "dollars are interesting," being in the threshold range of $30,000– $50,000.[39] These informal statements cannot be relied on to any appreciable extent, but they may indicate that the IRS will not impose intermediate sanctions on relatively small excess benefits, particularly where the parties acted in good faith.

INDIRECT EXCESS BENEFIT TRANSACTIONS

An excess benefit transaction is one that occurs *directly or indirectly* between an applicable tax-exempt organization and a disqualified person. One of the purposes of this phraseology is to prevent an applicable tax-exempt organization from causing a controlled entity to engage in an excess benefit transaction.

For example, public charity A wholly owns a for-profit subsidiary that performs publishing and other activities. One of A's very influential directors, Mr. Gamble, in a private meeting with A's president, Ms. Topp, stated that he desperately needed money to cover some large and mounting debts. President Topp felt sorry for Mr. Gamble but knew it would be improper for A to provide him with any of A's funds. However, she called the personnel manager of A's subsidiary and asked him to place Mr. Gamble on the subsidiary's payroll as a "special adviser," at an annual salary of $150,000. Mr. Gamble commenced receiving this salary on a monthly basis, although any duties performed by him were insubstantial.

The intermediate sanctions legislation, on its face, seemingly applies only to transactions involving tax-exempt organizations. However, in this case, President Topp caused the controlled subsidiary to engage in the transaction with Mr. Gamble, and the transaction created an excess benefit of $150,000 annually, because no meaningful services were being provided. This was an indirect excess benefit transaction.

Mr. Gamble is thus annually liable for the 25 percent initial excise tax on $150,000, or annual tax of $37,500. Mr. Gamble must also correct the transaction by returning the $150,000-per-year sum to the subsidiary. If this transaction is not timely corrected, Mr. Gamble becomes liable for an annual additional tax of $300,000.

Aside from the matter of interest and certain other amounts (and legal fees), Mr. Gamble, assuming a two-year audit, could have a total liability in this matter of $975,000—$675,000 in taxes and $300,000 owed to the subsidiary.

In addition, the IRS would undoubtedly take the position that President Topp, being an organization manager, participated in the excess benefit transaction knowing it to be such a transaction. This would cause her to be liable for an initial tax of 10 percent of the excess benefit, albeit up to a maximum of $10,000. Ten percent of the annual excess benefit would be $15,000; Topp's tax (the maximum penalty) would be $10,000.

HEALTH CARE INSTITUTIONS

It may be anticipated that hospitals and other health care institutions will be among the first of the public charitable entities to be involved in alleged excess benefit transactions. Indeed, for several reasons, it is quite likely that these institutions will be the first to experience entanglement in these rules.

Traditionally, health care institutions have been ensnarled in the private inurement rules because of transactions involving physicians on the medical staff. These transactions have usually involved forms of compensation and participation in joint ventures. A contemporary illustration is the matter of physician recruitment and retention. Issues also arise concerning the compensation of and other benefits flowing to the institution's chief executive officer. It may be anticipated that most transactions of this nature will be tested against the intermediate sanctions rules.

It has been the position of the IRS that every physician on a hospital's medical staff is, for that reason alone, an insider with respect to the hospital for purposes of application of the private inurement rules. This position is in the process of changing, in part because the legislative history of the intermediate sanctions rules states that physicians are disqualified persons only if they are in a position to exercise substantial influence over the affairs of an organization.[40]

GOVERNMENTAL AGENCIES

One of the issues being contemplated in the wake of enactment of the intermediate sanctions rules is their applicability to government agencies. These organizations are tax-exempt, but usually not because any specific provision in the Internal Revenue Code has accorded them tax-exempt status. Tax exemption is usually accorded these entities on the ground that (1) all of their income is excluded from tax as receipts derived by an instrumentality of government,[41] (2) the doctrine of intergovernmental immunity applies, or (3) their status is that of an integral part of the state.[42]

The general rule is that a governmental agency cannot be tax-exempt as a charitable organization[43] because it possesses certain characteristics that are inappropriate for a charity (basically, the police power, the power to tax, and the power of eminent domain). However, some governmental bodies have obtained rulings from the IRS that they qualify as charitable organizations. The rulings apply when these bodies have *clear counterparts* in the charitable sector—entities such as hospitals and schools. (Rulings of this nature are often sought so that, for purposes of the charitable contribution deduction or certain employee benefits programs, the charitable status of these entities is ensured.)

One of the issues that arises in this context is the extent to which governmental agencies must file annual information returns with the

IRS, as is generally required of "conventional" tax-exempt organizations. It has been clear for some time that governmental units, as such, are not required to file annual returns.[44] However, the position of the IRS is that, once a governmental unit receives a ruling that it is a tax-exempt organization, it has a "dual" status and its status as an exempt organization, as recognized in that ruling, triggers the requirement of filing returns, unless a specific exemption from that requirement is granted.

The intermediate sanctions rules present a similar quandary. These rules are applicable only with respect to *applicable tax-exempt organizations,* which generally are public charities and social welfare organizations.[45] Thus, it seems clear that governmental units that do not have a ruling as to recognition under either of these two provisions are not applicable tax-exempt organizations and thus are not caught up in the intermediate sanctions rules. This approach is reflected in the fact that an entity, as a general rule, cannot be regarded as a tax-exempt charitable entity without having filed with the IRS and obtained recognition to that end.[46]

There is an additional wrinkle in this context because of the precise wording of the definition of an applicable tax-exempt organization. This definition speaks of organizations which, without regard to any excess benefit, "would be" described as a tax-exempt public charity or social welfare organization.[47] The "would be" means that, absent the excess benefit, the entity would be described as one of these tax-exempt organizations.

However, it is unlikely that Congress meant to include governmental entities within the scope of intermediate sanctions. At the most, this definition of applicable tax-exempt organizations should be read to embrace only those governmental entities that are within the ambit of the clear counterpart doctrine, even if they do not have an IRS ruling recognizing their tax-exempt status as a charitable or social welfare organization. But even this interpretation is questionable, inasmuch as the "would be" almost certainly plays off only the reference to any excess benefit. The statute does not speak of an organization that "is" or "could be" so described.

Another approach would be to cause intermediate sanctions to be applicable only with respect to governmental entities that have rulings as to charitable status but not to those that may be eligible for such rulings but have not pursued them.

Governmental units that are outside the realm of the clear counterpart doctrine should assume they are not caught up in the intermediate sanctions scheme until and unless the IRS advises to the contrary. Those governmental units that have rulings recognizing them as charitable entities may want to assume they are applicable tax-exempt organizations (although that probably is not the intent of Congress) until the matter is clarified. (It is conceivable, but unlikely, that a governmental unit would be regarded as a social welfare organization.)

Admittedly, there is confusion on this point[48] and the matter should be clarified in tax regulations.

EXCESS BENEFIT INVOLVED

The initial intermediate sanctions penalty tax on disqualified persons is imposed at a rate equal to 25 percent of the excess benefit.[49] The term *excess benefit* means the difference between the value of the economic benefit provided by the exempt organization and the value of the consideration received for the provision of the benefit.[50] Thus, the amount of the initial tax can be computed once the values of the economic benefit provided and the consideration received are determined.[51]

This approach will often be simpler and more direct than the method employed in the most comparable of contexts—the private foundation self-dealing rules. In that setting, the taxes fall on the *amount involved*,[52] which, for the most part, is a vaguer concept. The phrase means the greater of the amount of money and the fair market value of the other property given, or the amount of money and the fair market value of the other property received.[53]

Despite the passage of more than 25 years, there is very little authority as to the meaning of the amount involved in the context of self-dealing and private foundations. The legislative history of the provision states that "the amount involved is the highest fair market value of the property during the period within which the transaction may be undone. This provision is intended to impose all market fluctuation risks upon the self-dealer who refuses to comply and to give the foundation the benefit of the best bargain it could have made at any time during the period."[54]

In one of the few court cases on the point, a disqualified person was found to be using his influence as a foundation trustee to steer foundation moneys to friends or associates without a quid pro quo to the foundation or its grantees; the amounts involved were held to be the amount of the grants themselves, as well as certain amounts paid that the court determined were for the personal benefit of the disqualified person.[55]

There are a small number of IRS determinations on the point:

1. A transfer of real property from a disqualified person to a private foundation was ruled an act of self-dealing; the amount involved

was the fair market value of the property on the date of the transfer.[56]

2. A transfer of assets by a disqualified person to a private foundation on the condition that it accept and repay the disqualified person's liabilities, consisting of a note payable to another disqualified person, was ruled an act of self-dealing; each payment by the foundation to the second disqualified person in satisfaction of the note payment requirements was also ruled self-dealing; the amount involved in the second instance was the amount of each of these payments.[57]

3. The collateralization with its assets by a private foundation of personal security trading accounts of disqualified persons was held to be an act of self-dealing; the amount involved was the fair market value of the use of the assets in the foundation's account as collateral and the fair amount of interest on that use of assets.[58]

The first two of these situations are relatively straightforward self-dealing transactions involving arrangements directly between a private foundation and a disqualified person. The rules of self-dealing also encompass the use of property for the benefit of a disqualified person and indirect self-dealing.[59] These two types of self-dealing somewhat correlate with the type of excess benefit transaction where an economic benefit is provided by an applicable tax-exempt organization (1) for the use of a disqualified person or (2) indirectly to a disqualified person by being provided directly to a nondisqualified person.[60] In the self-dealing context, the law as to the amount involved in these circumstances is almost nonexistent, thereby providing little authority for applicable intermediate sanctions in this setting. It is known that the concept of the amount involved goes beyond "pecuniary benefits"[61] and ventures into realms such as goodwill, reputation, and image enhancement.

This aspect of intermediate sanctions is likely to prove troublesome, if only because of the greater potential for excess benefit transactions in relation to acts of self-dealing. Exactly how will these amorphous benefits be valued? Or, more specifically, how will these vague forms of *excess benefit* be determined?

In one of its few pronouncements on the point, the IRS concluded that a bank was engaged in self-dealing when the private foundation for which it was the foundation manager invested in master notes and tax-exempt obligations negotiated by the bank solely for purposes of the investment; the transactions were held to enhance the reputation of the bank. The IRS was of the view that any benefit giving rise to "significantly increased 'goodwill' in a regulated industry, such as banking," is not an incidental and tenuous benefit,[62] and thus was self-dealing.[63] However, the IRS did not attempt to calculate the amount involved, namely, the value of this increased goodwill and reputation enhancement.

A subsequent case concerned a private foundation that made a loan to a client of its sole trustee, who was a lawyer in private practice. The IRS concluded that the lawyer utilized his position as the foundation manager to enhance his role as a lawyer by providing a valued client with a source of funds; by providing this service to a client, the lawyer was found to have given an economic benefit to himself by using the foundation's resources.[64] Again, the IRS did not endeavor to ascertain the economic value of this enhancement of the lawyer's role.

In a third set of circumstances, a private foundation collateralized the personal security trading accounts of disqualified persons. The benefits received by these persons were held to be a "disguised distribution" of the foundation's resources.[65] As noted above, this practice was held to be an act of self-dealing; the amount involved was the fair market value of the use of the assets in the foundation's account as collateral and the fair amount of interest on that use of assets. However, the IRS did not calculate these amounts.

In what appears to be the only other occasion when the IRS addressed this point, the benefit flowed to a nondisqualified person, albeit creating some benefit for a disqualified person. The IRS's lawyers essentially ducked the issue at that time, stating that more facts were needed. They conceded that "there may be some difficulty in placing a dollar amount upon that [intangible] value" received by the disqualified person; the sole suggestion provided was to "trace the path of the proceeds."[66]

HIGHEST FIDUCIARY STANDARDS

The intermediate sanctions additional tax on disqualified persons is imposed where an initial tax is imposed and the excess benefit involved is not timely "corrected."[67] The term *correction* means "undoing the excess benefit to the extent possible, and taking any additional measures necessary to place the organization in a financial position not worse than that in which it would be if the disqualified person were dealing under the highest fiduciary standards."[68] This phraseology is identical to that used in the private foundation self-dealing rules.[69]

The tax regulations in the self-dealing field state the minimum standards of correction where there has been a use of a private foundation's property by a disqualified person. Three outcomes are required (when applicable):

1. The transaction must be undone by terminating the use of the property;
2. The disqualified person must pay the foundation any excess of the fair market value of the use of the property over any amount paid by the disqualified person for the use until the date of termination; and
3. The disqualified person must pay a similar amount in connection with use of the property on or after the date of termination.[70]

Where the property in question is money, the "fair interest rate" is considered the fair market value of the use.[71]

There is almost no case law amplifying this standard. It is cited but not discussed in one case.[72] In the only court opinion on the point, the court suggested that the IRS did not follow the standard when it allowed a sales price for securities of $10.49 per share even though during the correction period there were offers at $14.00 per share.[73]

The IRS is of the view that the "highest fiduciary standards" incorporate equitable concepts of trust law, such as prevention of unjust enrichment. Thus, the IRS has written that "[i]f a disqualified person uses foundation funds and derives a profit, dealing under the highest fiduciary standards would require that both the borrowed funds and the profit go to the foundation."[74]

For example, suppose Sally, the commission-based fund-raiser, invested her $5 million windfall so that, during the investment period, it yielded $500,000. Thereafter, the IRS determined that the payment to her entailed an excess benefit transaction. The requirement of a *correction* means that Sally must return the $4,950,000 to the exempt organization. However, it also appears that Sally must pay some reasonable rate of interest (which may be less than the $500,000) to the tax-exempt organization. Indeed, the IRS pronouncement would indicate that Sally must disgorge all of her $500,000 investment profit. That outcome would require Sally to timely pay $5,450,000 to the exempt organization. If this amount is not paid within the correction period, she would, as noted above, be liable for an additional tax of $9,900,000, plus the initial tax of $1,237,500, plus the correction amount of $5,450,000, for an owed total of $15,350,000.[75]

This leads to another concept of trust law: compulsion to prevent unjust enrichment. The IRS is of the view that it has the authority to do this: it can require that the disqualified person transfer substantially appreciated property purchased with foundation funds as correction of the act of self-dealing.[76] An unknown is whether the IRS can compel rectification of an undue benefit, where the benefit was directly provided to a nondisqualified person who used it to generate a substantial benefit to a disqualified person.

Earlier versions of the intermediate sanctions rules included within the definition of *correction* the process of establishing safeguards to prevent future excess benefit transactions. Although the law does not statutorily embody that requirement, it would not be surprising to see the IRS require an applicable tax-exempt organization to embed certain safeguards in its policies and procedures to preclude recurrence of excess benefit transactions.

Consequently, in the setting of intermediate sanctions, this rule as to "highest fiduciary standards" is accompanied by these precedents. The rule, however, is not discussed in the legislative history of the sanctions.

NOTES

1. See Chapter Three.
2. E.g., "Tax Exempt!," 119 *U.S. News and World Report* (No. 13) 36 (Oct. 2, 1995).
3. E.g., *Birmingham Business College, Inc.* v. *Commissioner*, 276 F.2d 476 (5th Cir. 1960); *Mabee Petroleum Corporation* v. *United States*, 203 F.2d 872 (5th Cir. 1953).
4. IRC § 4958(f)(1)(A). See Chapter Two, text accompanied by notes 7–13.
5. IRC § 4958(f)(2). See Chapter Two, text accompanied by notes 35–40.
6. IRC § 4958(c)(1)(A). See Chapter One, text accompanied by notes 15–30.
7. This observation is not contained in any of the previous versions of the legislative history underlying the intermediate sanctions rules.
8. House Report at 56, note 5.
9. Schoenfeld and Repass, "'Intermediate Sanctions'—Issues, Pitfalls, and Protective Measures," 72 *Tax Notes* (No. 8) 1033 (Aug. 19, 1996).
10. See the discussion in Chapter Three, concerning the likelihood that the application of the intermediate sanctions rules will accelerate the development and clarity of principles of law on this topic.
11. IRC § 162; Reg. § 1.162-7. See *Kermit Fischer Foundation* v. *Commissioner*, 59 T.C.M. 898 (1990).
12. House Report at 56. Attached as Appendix E is an analysis prepared by William C. Mercer, Inc., an international human resources consulting firm specializing in the design and implementation of compensation and benefit programs, as to the process for determining the value and reasonableness of compensation.

13. *Id.*

14. One source of this information is compensation surveys for discrete fields (such as chief executive officers of hospitals, presidents of colleges, executive directors of associations, and trustees of private foundations). (The legislative history of intermediate sanctions references "independent compensation surveys by nationally recognized independent firms.") However, one difficulty with these surveys is that the compensation numbers (particularly for salaries) tend to be low, because payors on the high end of the compensation scales tend to not report the data. This is one reason why the IRS embraces the use of these surveys. Consequently, surveys of this nature can be useful but should be utilized appropriately.

15. This criterion is of particular use where a charitable or other organization is recruiting a particular individual. Examples of this would be a hospital seeking to induce a physician to join the medical staff, a research institution endeavoring to lure a prominent scientist to its ranks, or a college recruiting an individual to be a sports coach. The views of the IRS in this regard are reflected in proposed physician recruitment guidelines (Ann. 95-25, 1995-14 I.R.B. 10); in general, see Chapter 25 of Hyatt and Hopkins, *The Law of Tax-Exempt Healthcare Organizations* (New York: John Wiley & Sons, Inc., 1995).

16. This presumption is discussed in Chapter One, text accompanied by notes 31–38.

    A harbinger of things to come: The New York State Board of Regents removed 18 of the 19 trustees of Adelphi University, in part because of the Regents' view that the university's president was being paid too much and had too close of a relationship with many of the trustees (*The New York Times*, Feb. 11, 1997, p. A14).

17. *Elliotts, Inc.* v. *Commissioner,* 716 F.2d 1241 (9th Cir. 1983).

18. E.g., *Owensby & Kritikos, Inc.* v. *Commissioner,* 819 F.2d 1315 (5th Cir. 1987).

19. E.g., *Pepsi-Cola Bottling Co.* v. *Commissioner,* 528 F.2d 176 (10th Cir. 1975).

20. *Rapco, Inc.* v. *Commissioner,* 85 F.3d 950 (2d Cir. 1996).

21. Subsequently, the U.S. Tax Court concluded that an individual who was paid, in a year, $1,777,700 should have been paid no more than $700,000 (*Leonard Pipeline Contractors, Ltd.* v. *Commissioner,* 72 T.C.M. 83 (1996)).

22. IRC § 4958(c)(2). See Chapter One, text accompanied by notes 23–27.

23. See Chapter Three, text accompanied by notes 40–49.

24. See Chapter One, text accompanied by note 25.

25. IRS Gen. Couns. Mem. 39862 (Nov. 22, 1991).

26. House Report at 56.

27. IRS Gen. Couns. Mem. 38283 (Feb. 15, 1980). Comparable plans were considered in IRS Gen. Couns. Mem. 35869 (June 21, 1974), 35865 (June 21, 1974), and 32518 (Feb. 20, 1963).

    This is an area where language is a barrier, particularly for those who believe that a nonprofit organization is not supposed to generate profits.

That is not the law (see Chapter Three, pages 53–55). The IRS has recognized this "semantic anomaly" (IRS Gen. Couns. Mem. 38283).

28. This basically entails adherence to the standards applicable to profit-sharing plans generally (IRC Chapter 1, Subchapter D, and Chapter 43; Employee Retirement Income Security Act, Title I). The trusts underlying these plans usually qualify under IRC § 401(a).

29. E.g., IRS Gen. Couns. Mem. 35638 (Jan. 28, 1974) and 36918 (Nov. 11, 1976).

30. This position can be found in the three general counsel memoranda referenced in *supra* note 27.

31. IRC § 4958(c)(2).

32. E.g., IRS Gen. Couns. Mem. 39674 (Oct. 23, 1987).

33. IRS Gen. Couns. Mem. 38905 (Oct. 6, 1982).

34. These organizations are tax-exempt by reason of IRC § 501(c)(2).

35. IRS Gen. Couns. Mem. 32453 (Nov. 30, 1962).

36. *Id.*

37. Rev. Rul. 69-383, 1969-2 C.B. 113; IRS Gen. Couns. Mem. 36918 (Nov. 11, 1976), 35638 (Jan. 28, 1974), and 31081 (Jan. 26, 1959).

38. IRS Gen. Couns. Mem. 38905 (Oct. 6, 1982).

39. "Panelists Sound Warning on Intermediate Sanctions," 3 *EOTR Weekly* (No. 13) 99 (Sept. 23, 1996).

40. House Report at 58, note 12.

41. IRC § 115.

42. For example, only recently, an issue concerned the tax-exempt status of trusts that operate state prepaid tuition payment programs. The IRS has refused to accord these trusts recognition of tax exemption by reason of IRC § 501(c)(3) on the ground that the disbursements of funds to eligible beneficiaries (students) constitute either private inurement or private benefit to the beneficiaries and/or their parents. The U.S. Court of Appeals for the Sixth Circuit held that these trusts are exempt from federal income tax because they are integral parts of the state (*Michigan* v. *United States*, 40 F.3d 817 (6th Cir. 1994)). For tax years ending after August 20, 1996, qualified state tuition payment trusts are tax-exempt by reason of IRC § 529 (added by § 1806 of the Small Business Job Protection Act of 1996 (P.L. 104-188, 104th Cong., 2d Sess. (1996)).

43. That is, an IRC § 501(c)(3) entity.

44. See Chapter Five, text accompanied by note 6.

45. IRC § 4958(e). See Chapter One, text accompanied by notes 4–14.

46. IRC § 508(a). See Chapter Five, text accompanied by note 34.

47. IRC § 4958(e)(1).

48. E.g., "Practitioners Say Intermediate Sanctions Law May Apply to Section 115 Entities," *Daily Tax Report* (No. 164) G-2 (Aug. 23, 1996).

49. IRC § 4958(a)(1). See Chapter One, text accompanied by notes 54–55.

50. IRC § 4958(c)(1)(B).

51. The amount of an excess benefit is also used in computing the tax on organization managers (IRC § 4958(a)(2)) and the additional tax (IRC § 4958(b)).

52. IRC § 4941(a) and (b).

53. IRC § 4941(e)(2).

54. H. Rep. No. 91-413, 91st Cong., 1st Sess., part I at 23 (1969); S. Rep. No. 91-552, 91st Cong., 1st Sess., at 33 (1969).

55. *Moody* v. *Commissioner,* 69 T.C.M. 2517 (1995).

56. Tech. Adv. Mem. 8644001 (May 30, 1986).

57. Tech. Adv. Mem. 9137006 (May 31, 1991).

58. Tech. Adv. Mem. 9627001 (Nov. 10, 1995).

59. IRC § 4941(d)(1)(E).

60. IRC § 4958(c)(1)(A).

61. *Estate of Reis* v. *Commissioner,* 87 T.C. 1016, 1023 (1987).

62. In the private foundation setting, there is no self-dealing if the benefit provided to a disqualified person is incidental or tenuous (Reg. § 53.4941(d)-2(f)(2)).

63. IRS Gen. Couns. Mem. 39107 (Dec. 23, 1983). This viewpoint was reaffirmed in IRS Gen. Couns. Mem. 39632 (May 12, 1987).

64. Tech. Adv. Mem. 8719004 (Feb. 3, 1987).

65. Tech. Adv. Mem. 9627001 (Nov. 30, 1995).

66. IRS Gen. Couns. Mem. 39632 (May 12, 1987).

67. IRC § 4958(b).

68. IRC § 4958(f)(6).

69. IRC § 4941(e)(3).

70. Reg. § 53.4941(e)-1(c)(4)(i).

71. IRS Gen. Couns. Mem. 37702 (Sept. 29, 1978).

72. *Deluxe Check Printers, Inc.* v. *United States,* 14 Cl. Ct. 782 (1988).

73. *Oliff* v. *Exchange International Corporation,* 669 F.2d 1162, 1168 (7th Cir. 1980), *cert. denied,* 450 U.S. 915 (1981).

74. IRS Gen. Couns. Mem. 37702 (Sept. 29, 1978).

75. Whether the IRS will require this type of tracing of income from assets remains to be seen. There will be situations where assets from an excess benefit transaction and other assets are so commingled and coinvested that one will not be able to determine which assets produced which gain.

76. IRS Gen. Couns. Mem. 37702 (Sept. 29, 1978).

CHAPTER FIVE

Expanded Reporting and Disclosure Requirements

I ntermediate sanctions became part of the federal tax law upon enactment of the Taxpayer Bill of Rights 2.[1] However, that legislation also brought other federal tax law requirements directly applicable to tax-exempt organizations: an expansion of the contents of annual information returns and of certain disclosure requirements, and of the penalties underlying these bodies of law.

EXPANDED REPORTING REQUIREMENTS

Nearly every tax-exempt organization is required to file an annual information return with the IRS.[2] Exempted from this requirement are (1) churches, integrated auxiliaries of churches, and conventions or associations of churches; (2) most charitable organizations, instrumentalities of the United States, and certain fraternal organizations, where their annual gross receipts are normally no more than $5,000; and (3) religious orders.[3] Under the authority of the IRS to grant exemptions from the reporting requirement in the interest of efficient administration of the internal revenue laws, the IRS has exempted (1) many organizations that normally have gross receipts not in excess of $25,000;[4]

(2) certain foreign organizations that normally do not have gross receipts in excess of $25,000 from sources in the United States;[5] (3) governmental units and tax-exempt affiliates of them;[6] and (4) certain church-affiliated organizations exclusively engaged in managing funds or maintaining retirement programs.[7]

For most exempt organizations, this return is filed on Form 990. An organization may file a simpler (two-page) annual return in a year in which it has gross receipts of less than $100,000 and total assets of less than $250,000 at the end of the year; this return is filed on Form 990-EZ.[8]

The Form 990 (and 990-EZ) statutory rules mandate annual submission of a tax-exempt organization's items of gross income, receipts, disbursements, and certain lobbying expenses.[9] Form 990 also requires the following items of information from exempt organizations obligated to file annual returns:

- Expenses stated by function;
- Program service accomplishments;
- Balance sheets;
- List of directors, officers, and key employees;
- Analysis of income-producing activities;
- Relationship of activities to accomplishment of exempt purposes;
- Information concerning taxable subsidiaries; and
- A variety of other items of information.

Also, as stated prior to the enactment of the intermediate sanctions legislation, the Form 990 rules mandate submission of the following items of information, for the year involved, by tax-exempt charitable organizations:[10]

- Gross income;
- Expenses attributable to gross income;
- Disbursements for tax-exempt purposes;
- Balance sheet showing assets, liabilities, and net worth;
- Contributions received;
- Names and addresses of substantial contributors;
- Names and addresses of, and compensation and other payments to, the organization's managers and highly compensated employees;
- Certain information concerning lobbying; and

- Certain information concerning transfers to other tax-exempt organizations.[11]

Form 990 also requires:

- Compensation paid to principal independent contractors;
- Identification of the organization's public charity status; and
- Certain information concerning private schools.

As part of the intermediate sanctions legislative package, these filing requirements for public charitable organizations have been expanded. For tax years beginning after July 30, 1996 (the date of enactment of the intermediate sanctions legislation),[12] the following additional information must be provided to the IRS:[13]

1. The respective amounts (if any) of the taxes paid by the organization during the tax year because of excess expenditures to influence legislation,[14] because of disqualifying lobbying expenditures of certain organizations,[15] and/or because of expenditures for political campaign activities;[16]
2. The respective amounts (if any) of the taxes paid by the organization, or any disqualified person with respect to the organization, during the tax year by reason of the intermediate sanctions rules;[17]
3. Information the IRS may require with respect to any excess benefit transaction; and
4. Information the IRS may require with respect to disqualified persons.[18]

Tax-exempt social welfare organizations must include on their annual information return any information concerning the last three of the above four categories of information.[19]

Thus, it cannot accurately be said that intermediate sanctions are merely a dilemma for disqualified persons of public charities and social welfare organizations. Participation in an excess benefit transaction can have direct, adverse consequences for an applicable tax-exempt organization as well. For the most part, these consequences include negative, perhaps financially harmful, publicity. The risk of receiving adverse publicity has been greatly expanded, now that the details of excess benefit transactions must be described in the annual information return, and any information in the return will have increased availability and wider dissemination.[20]

The IRS, on its own initiative, is in the process of implementing a plan to further expand the scope of annual information return reporting regarding:

- Changes to an organization's governing board;
- Change of accounting firm;
- Information concerning the professional fund-raising fees paid by an organization; and
- Aggregate payments (by related entities) in excess of $100,000 to the highest-paid employees.

The legislative history underlying this legislation encourages the IRS to implement this plan.[21]

INCREASE IN RETURN PENALTIES

Adoption of the intermediate sanctions brought an increase in the penalties for failure to file complete and timely annual information returns. These increased penalties are applicable to returns for tax years ending on or after July 30, 1996 (the date of enactment of the legislation).[22]

Under the law in effect before those tax years, a tax-exempt organization that failed to file a complete and accurate annual information return was subject to a penalty of $10 for each day during which the failure continued.[23] For any one return, there was a maximum penalty of the lesser of $5,000 or 5 percent of the organization's gross receipts for the year.[24] No penalty is imposed where it is shown that the failure to file a complete return was due to reasonable cause.[25] (This latter rule was not adjusted by the new law.)

In general, the new penalties are a doubling of the previous ones. The penalty that was $10 per day is, as of the effective date, generally $20 per day.[26] Likewise, the $5,000 limitation is, as of the effective date, $10,000.[27] (The alternative 5 percent threshold was not altered.)

However, there is, as of the effective date, a much larger penalty on organizations with gross receipts in excess of $1 million for a year. In this circumstance, the per-day penalty is $100 and the maximum penalty is $50,000.[28]

Specifically, these penalties can apply where there has been a failure to (1) timely file a return[29] or (2) include any of the information required to be shown on a return or show the correct information.[30]

A tax-exempt organization that, without reasonable cause, omits material information and therefore files an incomplete information return on Form 990, has failed to file a return for purposes of this penalty and for purposes of starting the period of limitations (generally, three years) as to assessment and collection of tax.[31]

Most categories of tax-exempt organizations are not required to file an application for recognition of tax-exempt status, and obtain a determination letter from the IRS as to exempt status, to be tax-exempt.[32] Social welfare organizations are one of these categories. Nonetheless, many of these organizations voluntarily seek recognition of tax-exempt status from the IRS.

However, to be tax-exempt, nearly all charitable organizations[33] must obtain recognition of exempt status from the IRS.[34] The only organizations that are exempt from this requirement are (1) churches, interchurch organizations of local units of a church, integrated auxiliaries of churches, and conventions or associations of churches; (2) organizations (other than private foundations) that normally do not have more than $5,000 in annual gross receipts; and (3) organizations (other than private foundations) that are covered by a group exemption letter.[35]

There is no specific penalty for the filing of an application for recognition of tax-exempt status that contains inaccurate statements or omissions of material fact. However, these applications are signed under penalty of perjury, and the ruling is only as valid as the material facts on which it is based.

EXPANDED DISCLOSURE REQUIREMENTS

Tax-exempt organizations are required to allow public inspection at the organization's principal office (and certain regional or district offices) of their annual information returns for the three most recent tax years.[36] Tax-exempt organizations are also required to allow public inspection of: the organization's application to the IRS for recognition of tax-exempt status (usually, Form 1023 or 1024), the IRS determination letter, and certain related documents.[37] The organization must allow the requester to take notes while inspecting the returns. The law does not require the organization to provide a copy of any of these documents to a requester.

Upon written request to the IRS, members of the general public are permitted to inspect annual information returns of tax-exempt organizations, and applications for recognition of exempt status (and related documents), at the National Office of the IRS in Washington, DC. A person who submits a written request is notified by the IRS when the material is available for inspection at the National Office. Notes may be taken of the material open for inspection, photographs may be taken with the person's own equipment, or copies of the material may be obtained from the IRS for a fee.[38] Copies of these documents will be provided by the IRS by mail.

Tax-exempt organizations that fail to make their annual returns and applications for recognition of tax exemption available for public inspection are, under present law, subject to a penalty of $10 for each day the failure continues.[39] The maximum penalty with respect to any one return is $5,000. There is no limitation with respect to applications. For willfully failing to make an annual information return or exemption application available for public inspection, the penalty imposed is $1,000 per return or application.[40]

There is a penalty for failure to allow inspection of any return or application for recognition of exemption.[41] Under prior law, the penalty was $10 per day for each day during which the failure continued, with the total penalty not to exceed $5,000. The new law is that any person failing to allow inspection of annual returns must pay $20 per day for each day the failure continues, up to a total of $10,000.[42] Any person failing to allow inspection of an organization's application for recognition of tax exemption must pay $20 per day for each day the failure continues.[43]

As an expansion of the disclosure requirement,[44] if an individual makes a request at the principal, regional, or district office of a tax-exempt organization, copies of the following documents must be provided to the individual:

- One or more of the organization's three most recent annual information returns; and/or
- The organization's application for recognition of exemption (together with a copy of any supporting papers and any document issued by the IRS in response).[45]

This request will have to be made in person or in writing. The copy of the return will have to be provided without charge, other than a reasonable fee for any reproduction and mailing costs.

When the request is made in person, the copy of the return will have to be provided "immediately." Thus, exempt organizations will have to maintain a supply of copied annual returns to hand out upon request.[46] When the request is made in writing, a copy of the return will have to be provided within 30 days.[47]

The requirement as to the provision of copies of annual information returns will be inapplicable in two instances:[48]

1. Where the organization has made the returns "widely available"; or
2. Where the IRS determines that the request is part of a "harassment campaign and that compliance with such request is not in the public interest." The organization must apply to the IRS for this determination.

Both of these exceptions are directed to be the subject of IRS regulations. The effective date of these rules is for requests made on or after the 60th day after the Department of the Treasury first issues these regulations.[49] Until that time, the existing law governs the manner in which a tax-exempt organization must allow inspection of its annual information returns and exemption application by the public.

Again, the penalty will be significantly increased. The present-day penalty for willful failure to comply with the public inspection rules is $1,000.[50] However, for requests made on or after the 60th day following issuance by the Department of the Treasury of the final version of the antiharassment regulations,[51] this penalty becomes $5,000.[52] The legislative history of this law states that the House Committee on Ways and Means "expects" that tax-exempt organizations will "comply voluntarily" with the public inspection provisions prior to the issuance of the regulations.[53]

FUTURE GUIDANCE

The IRS will be issuing guidance, in the form of interpretations of some of these rules, particularly ways in which an organization can qualify for the disclosure exemption by making the relevant documents widely available.[54] On September 12, 1996, the IRS invited comments on these rules.[55] At that time, it was suggested that suitable alternatives for qualifying for this exemption could include electronic dissemination through the Internet or other electronic databases, depositing copies at public libraries, or providing copies to third-party organizations that will make the documents available to the public for a reasonable fee. The IRS also invited comments with respect to how these methods could satisfy requests made in person or in writing. The deadline for the submission of comments was November 12, 1996.

NOTES

1. See Chapter One, note 1.
2. IRC § 6033(a)(1). See *Tax-Exempt Organizations,* Chapter 37, § 4.
3. IRC § 6033(a)(2)(A).
4. Rev. Proc. 83-23, 1983-1 C.B. 687.
5. Rev. Proc. 94-17, 1994-1 C.B. 579.
6. Rev. Proc. 95-48, 1995-2 C.B. 418.
7. Rev. Proc. 96-10, 1996-2 I.R.B. 8.
8. Tax-exempt charitable organizations (those described in IRC § 501(c)(3), other than private foundations) are also required to file Schedule A as part of the annual return filing requirements. This schedule must accompany both Form 990 and Form 990-EZ.
9. IRC § 6033(a)(1) and (e).
10. These requirements are applicable with respect to all charitable organizations, other than those exempt from the requirement (see *supra* notes 3–7). Private foundations, which file an annual information return on Form 990-PF, are subject to an additional set of statutory requirements (IRC § 6033(c)).
11. IRC § 6033(b)(1)–(9). Some of this information is submitted on Schedule A (see *supra* note 8).
12. Act § 1312(c).
13. IRC § 6033(b)(10)–(13).
14. IRC § 4911 (excise tax of 25 percent on excess lobbying expenditures, paid by charitable organizations that have elected (IRC § 501(h)) the safe- harbor rules known as the expenditure test). This tax is the subject of Chapter 14, § 4, of *Tax-Exempt Organizations*
15. IRC § 4912 (an excise tax of 5 percent of lobbying expenditures, where tax exemption of the charitable organization to which the substantial-part test applies is lost for excess lobbying; similar tax on the organization's managers who agreed to the lobbying expenditures knowing that they were likely to result in the revocation). This tax is the subject of Chapter 14, § 9, of *Tax-Exempt Organizations.*
16. IRC § 4955 (a 10 percent initial tax on political expenditures; a 2½ percent initial tax on the organization's managers who knew the expenditure was a political one; an additional tax of 100 percent on the organization; and an additional tax on management of 50 percent). This tax is the subject of Chapter 15, § 7, of *Tax-Exempt Organizations.*

   There is a fourth tax regime to which charitable and other tax-exempt organizations may be subject for engaging in political activities: that of IRC § 527(f)(1). These activities include undertakings other than involvement in political campaigns, such as attempts to influence presidential nominations to the Cabinet or courts. This tax is the subject of

Chapter 33, § 6, of *Tax-Exempt Organizations*. Oddly, the expanded reporting requirements do not encompass the payment of this tax.

17. The statute on this point (IRC § 6033(b)(11)) specifically requires reporting of the "respective amounts (if any) of the taxes *paid by the organization, or any disqualified person with respect to such organization . . .*" (emphasis added). The italicized reference is not clear; the intermediate sanctions regime does not contain any taxes imposed on an applicable tax-exempt organization. This language either refers to situations where an applicable tax-exempt organization reimbursed a disqualified person for an excess benefits transactions tax (thereby effectively paying the tax) or it is an error reflective of earlier versions of intermediate sanctions legislation (see Chapter Two, text accompanied by notes 94–97).

18. This requirement is not intended to limit the IRS's general authority (IRC § 6033(a)(1)) to require, for the purpose of carrying out the internal revenue laws, information on annual returns filed by tax-exempt organizations. House Report at 60.

19. IRC § 6033(f).

20. See the text accompanied by *infra* notes 36–49.

21. House Report at 60, note 16.

22. Act § 1314(c).

23. IRC § 6652(c)(1)(A) (prior law).

24. *Id.*

25. IRC § 6652(c)(3).

26. IRC § 6652(c)(1)(A).

27. *Id.*

28. *Id.*, last sentence.

29. IRC § 6652(c)(1)(A)(i).

30. IRC § 6652(c)(1)(A)(ii).

31. Rev. Rul. 77-162, 1977-1 C.B. 400.

32. The tax exemption recognition process is the subject of Chapter 32 of *Tax-Exempt Organizations*.

33. That is, organizations described in IRC § 501(c)(3).

34. IRC § 508(a).

35. IRC § 508(c); Reg. § 1.508-1(a)(3)(i).

36. IRC § 6104(e). This disclosure rule is the subject of Chapter 37, § 6, of *Tax-Exempt Organizations*. There are additional rules in this regard for private foundations (*id.*, Chapter 37, § 5).

37. *Tax-Exempt Organizations*, Chapter 37.

38. Reg. §§ 301.6104(a)-6 and 301.6104(b)-1.

39. IRC § 6652(c)(1)(C).

40. IRC § 6685.

41. IRC § 6652(c)(1)(C) and (D).

42. IRC § 6652(c)(1)(C) (as amended).

43. IRC § 6652(c)(1)(D) (as amended). The increase in this penalty and the one reflected in *supra* note 42 were intended to be made as part of the intermediate sanctions legislation; however, the revisions were inadvertently omitted. Congress corrected this omission by adding the penalty revisions by enactment of § 1704(s) of the Small Business Job Protection Act of 1996, P.L. 104-188, 104th Cong., 2d Sess. (1996), 110 Stat. 1755. This legislation was signed into law on August 20, 1996.

44. The foregoing requirements will, once the new law becomes effective (see *infra* note 49), be the subject of IRC § 6104(e)(1)(A)(i).

45. IRC § 6104(e)(1)(A)(ii) (not yet effective; see note 49 *infra*). The IRS provided a brief summary of these rules in Notice 96-48, 1996-39 I.R.B. 8.

46. A tax-exempt organization should not wait until a request of this nature is made, and then keep the requesting individual waiting while the appropriate return (or returns) is located and a copy made. This practice would be a violation of the rule that the copied return is to be provided "immediately."

47. IRC § 6104(e)(1)(A), final two sentences (not yet effective; see *infra* note 49).

48. IRC § 6104(e)(3) (not yet effective; see *infra* note 49).

49. Act § 1313(c).

50. IRC § 6685.

51. See the text accompanied by *supra* note 49.

52. Prospective IRC § 6685.

53. House Report at 61.

54. See the text accompanied by *supra* note 48.

55. IRS Notice 96-48, *supra* note 45.

CHAPTER SIX

Planning for Compliance

Applicable tax-exempt organizations, and the disqualified persons with respect to them, should attend to a number of tasks in the wake of enactment of intermediate sanctions. Here is a checklist of those tasks:

- The management of an applicable tax-exempt organization (again, a public charity or social welfare organization) should prepare and keep current a list of all disqualified persons with respect to the organization. A rather vast network can be involved: disqualified persons' ancestors, spouses, children, grandchildren, great grandchildren, brothers, sisters, brothers and sisters of spouses, and spouses of the foregoing, not to mention corporations, partnerships, trusts, or estates in which disqualified persons and family members have a meaningful economic interest. Care may be required to avoid an inadvertent triggering of intermediate sanctions penalties.

- In determining who is a disqualified person, titles may be of little significance. The trick is to determine who has "substantial influence" over the affairs of an applicable tax-exempt organization. Of particular consequence are key employees and influential vendors of services (such as lawyers and fund-raisers).

- The management of an applicable tax-exempt organization should maintain an inventory of all transactions with disqualified

106

persons. Remember that the intermediate sanctions rules apply with respect to all transactions occurring on or after September 14, 1995. To this end, the organization should implement a conflict-of-interest policy.

- The key to compliance in this area is documentation. When an applicable tax-exempt organization enters into a transaction with a disqualified person, the record (such as minutes of a board of directors meeting) should be clear as to why the transaction is necessary, appropriate, and/or important. The criteria underlying the rebuttable presumption (see below) should be followed to the extent possible (even if the presumption is not to be utilized). The point is, the reasonableness of all benefits should be documented. Two critical elements are: (1) levels of compensation and (2) value of property. Also important are the rental value as to a lease and the terms of a borrowing transaction. The criteria followed in setting these items should be documented. Independent expert advice (such as a compensation study or a property appraisal) is highly essential. Even if this documentation does not shift the burden of proof to the government (see below), it will reduce the likelihood of an IRS finding of an excess benefit.

- The concept of an excess benefit rests on the *value* assigned to that benefit. The cost to the applicable tax-exempt organization, or to an entity it controls, is irrelevant. Thus, what may appear to be an incidental benefit (because the cost is low or nothing) may be, for intermediate sanctions penalty purposes, a substantial (excess) economic benefit.

- There should never be an assumption that a compensation package paid to a disqualified person by an applicable tax-exempt organization is reasonable just because the same one was paid to a predecessor. Each individual's compensation must be reasonable based on the particular facts and circumstances, including his or her education, training, and experience.

- An applicable tax-exempt organization should, at a minimum, consider utilization of the rebuttable presumption as to reasonableness of compensation and property values. The purpose of this presumption is to shift to the government the burden of proving the existence of an excess benefit. The price for the presumption may be too great (such as by making the board entirely independent of the disqualified person involved in the transaction). But at least the possibility of a structuring or restructuring of the board should be entertained.

- The rebuttable presumption may be utilized where the arrangement with a disqualified person was approved by an independent board of directors or trustees (or committee thereof). If the committee option is selected, the members of the committee must all be members of the board. It is not sufficient for the board members to appoint a committee of individuals who are not trustees or directors of the organization. (This approach seemed available under previous versions of the intermediate sanctions legislation.)

- There was a one-time window of opportunity as to this presumption. Parties to transactions entered into after September 13, 1995, and before January 1, 1997, were entitled to rely on the presumption if, within a reasonable period (such as 90 days) after entering into a transaction, the parties satisfied the criteria giving rise to the presumption.

- At the same time, too much can be made of this presumption. It is, after all, rebuttable. Thus, even if a good case is made that an economic benefit provided to a disqualified person is not excessive, the IRS can retaliate with "sufficient contrary evidence." For example, as to a compensation arrangement, the data relied on by an organization may not have been for a functionally comparable position.

- An applicable tax-exempt organization should identify its organization managers. Again, titles may be of little significance; for example, key employees are treated as officers.

- If an economic benefit provided to a disqualified person is to be treated as compensation to him or her, it must be identified as such at the outset and (except in the case of nontaxable fringe benefits) reported as compensation on the appropriate IRS form(s).

- Management of an applicable tax-exempt organization should be wary about entering into compensation transactions that, in whole or in part, are revenue-sharing arrangements, including incentive compensation plans and commission-based fund-raising. This caution should be particularly acute until the extent to which the Treasury Department and the IRS will be rewriting the rules in this area can be determined.

- An applicable tax-exempt organization may have a ruling from the IRS that a particular revenue-sharing arrangement—commission-based compensation, incentive compensation, or profit-sharing plan—is allowable. Prodded by Congress, the IRS may alter its position as to one or more of these arrangements. One or more of these rulings may be nullified by a future policy shift.

- An applicable tax-exempt organization should be cautious in implementing a program of reimbursement and/or insurance for intermediate sanctions taxes. First, it is essential that the reimbursement and/or payment of insurance premiums be included in disqualified persons' compensation; if it is not, that alone is an excess benefit. Second, these items must be added to other compensation paid to disqualified persons in determining reasonableness. Third, particularly in the case of additional taxes, care must be exercised to avoid situations where reimbursement of the tax triggers another round of excess benefit. Also, the purchase of this type of insurance—protection against penalties on disqualified persons because of excess benefit insider transactions—may be awkward for some organizations, particularly charitable ones.

- Organization managers should be careful in approving transactions between the applicable tax-exempt organization and disqualified persons. If an excess benefit is found and the manager knew of it (as that term will be defined), the manager can be personally taxed.

- In most instances, the management of an applicable tax-exempt organization cannot do indirectly what it cannot do directly. Thus, a disqualified person should not be given an excess benefit out of the resources of an affiliated entity, such as a controlled corporation.

- Some applicable tax-exempt membership organizations may benefit from forthcoming IRS guidance as to exclusion of membership benefits from the realm of excess benefit transactions. Thus, a benefit of this nature provided to a disqualified person will not generate an intermediate sanctions penalty if the benefit is also generally available to all members of the organization.

- An excess benefit transaction involving an applicable tax-exempt organization must be described in the organization's annual information return (Form 990), which is a public document. Thus, management of the organization will want to describe the circumstances concerning provision of the excess benefit in phraseology that is most favorable (within the bounds of the truth) to the organization.

- Under present law, a tax-exempt organization is required to make copies of its annual returns (and its application for recognition of tax exemption) available to anyone for review. Forthcoming law will require that, in general, copies of these documents will have to be provided to those who request them. However, Congress has said that, in the interim, it "expects" organizations to "voluntarily" comply with the coming rules. Management of a tax-exempt organization will have to decide whether to adhere to this expectation.

• The management of applicable tax-exempt organizations should remain vigilant for guidance from the IRS and other sources as to interpretation of the intermediate sanctions law. Present indications are that the first of the IRS guidance—probably in a question-and-answer format—will appear by the close of 1997.[1]

• Intermediate sanctions should be kept in perspective. The law as to private inurement and private benefit has not been repealed. Even if a transaction is not an excess benefit transaction, it may entail private inurement or benefit that may endanger the organization's tax-exempt status. Also, tax exemption can be jeopardized even in the event of intermediate sanctions, if excess benefit arrangements are substantial.

NOTE

1. "Panelists Sound Warnings on Intermediate Sanctions," 3 *EOTR Weekly* (No. 13) 99 (Sept. 23, 1996).

Epilogue

Just about everyone loves to see a villain get his or her just punishment—and not simply in the movies. Particularly in recent years, the general public seems to be delighted when the villain is an insider whom the IRS has caught plundering a nonprofit organization. An obvious purpose of the intermediate sanctions legislation is to cause would-be "villains" to be dissuaded from plundering charitable and social welfare organizations or, if they do so, to force them to pay a very high price.

In the Prologue, readers were introduced to Jack Dunlop, Betty McGowan, Howard McKenzie, and Mary Adams—four honest individuals who are representative of the thousands of people throughout the nation who work hard each day on behalf of tax-exempt organizations. Jack, Betty, Howard, and Mary each eventually discovered, to his or her surprise, that the new intermediate sanctions legislation can not only be used to catch plundering villains, but can also occasionally trip up even the most well-intentioned persons.

JACK DUNLOP

As will be recalled, Jack Dunlop was a young and very influential chief executive officer of a charitable hospital. He demanded his annual salary of $300,000 primarily because that was the salary his predecessor received. The fact that he lacked his predecessor's education and experience was overlooked. Moreover, the hospital's board of directors shirked their responsibility by never reviewing appropriate salary data in order to determine, in some objective way, whether Jack's salary was reasonable. An IRS agent auditing the hospital for a two-year period after September 14, 1995, determined, after comparison data were compiled, that a reasonable salary for someone with Jack's credentials was $200,000 (not $300,000) per year. The agent also determined that Jack was a disqualified person because he exercised "substantial influence" over the affairs of the organization. If the IRS agent is correct in her findings, Jack could be forced to pay an excise tax equal to 25 percent of the "excess benefit" he received (that is, 25 percent of the amount that his salary exceeded the reasonable compensation figure of $200,000 calculated by the IRS). In Jack's case, this amounts to $25,000 in tax for each year under audit, for a two-year total of $50,000. In addition, jack must "undo" the transaction to the extent possible, which means he must give back to the hospital $100,000, plus interest, for each year under audit. This results in a refund to the hospital of $200,000 for the two years in question. If Jack fails to pay the tax and undo the transaction by the end of the "taxable period" (that is, the earliest of the date of mailing of the notice of deficiency with respect to the initial tax or the date on which the initial tax is assessed), Jack will have an additional tax equal to 200 percent of the excess benefit involved. In Jack's case, this would amount to an additional $400,000 in tax.

Upon receiving a notice of deficiency for the initial excise tax of $50,000, Jack immediately contacted a lawyer specializing in the law of tax-exempt organizations. This lawyer contacted the IRS agent in charge of Jack's case and requested a meeting. At that meeting, persuasive evidence was offered on a number of points. First, the lawyer established that both Jack and the hospital's board of directors truly believed that it was reasonable for Jack to be paid what the predecessor in his particular position was paid. In fact, the lawyer presented some long-standing IRS authority listing the pay of a predecessor as one of many factors that the IRS might rely on in determining whether compensation is reasonable. The lawyer also found that typical salary surveys for positions like Jack's did not specify the experience of those responding to the survey; instead, salaries were organized according to job title and size of organization. Thus, the lawyer argued, it is unlikely that Jack or the board of directors could have readily determined that Jack was overpaid, even if a reputable salary survey had been reviewed for comparison purposes. Additionally, the lawyer established that, despite Jack's general influence within the organization, his compensation was voted on by an independent board of directors in an arm's-length manner. Indeed, Jack was not allowed to be present in the room during the discussion of his compensation or during the vote to approve the compensation. Based on these facts, the lawyer asked that Jack's excise tax be abated because the excessive compensation was due to reasonable cause and not to willful neglect.

This request is still under consideration by the IRS. Even if Jack prevails on his request for abatement, however, he will undoubtedly have to pay back the $100,000 per year in excessive compensation, which will wipe out his savings and probably force him to take out a second mortgage on his home.

There is a key lesson to be learned from Jack's predicament: Never assume that the compensation received by a disqualified person is reasonable just because it is similar to the amount a predecessor received for those same duties. Each individual must be paid reasonable compensation based on a wide number of facts and circumstances, including the person's relevant education and experience.

BETTY McGOWAN

In the Prologue, readers also learned that Betty McGowan was an influential director of one of the region's largest museums. Betty's stepbrother was quite the salesman and had persuaded the museum's board of directors to rent the property for the museum's newest display building from his partnership for $700,000 per year. The partners consisted of Betty, her husband, her stepbrother, and her stepbrother's wife. Each of the partners owned an equal-profit interest in the partnership. Unfortunately, the board had not checked with anyone to determine the true fair rental value of the property, and Betty later learned from her stepbrother that the true rental value may be no more than $500,000 annually.

An IRS agent read about the rental transaction in a newspaper and audited the museum for a two-year period after 1995. The agent concluded that the annual fair rental value of the building was $500,000 (not $700,000) per year. The agent also determined that Betty was a disqualified person with respect to the museum because she has substantial influence over the museum's affairs. Although the museum contracted with a partnership and not with Betty, a partnership also can be a disqualified person if a disqualified person (or a member of the family of such person) owns more than a 35 percent profits interest in the partnership. As noted above, Betty is a disqualified person, but she owns only 25 percent of the partnership profits interest. However, Betty's husband, her stepbrother, and her stepbrother's wife are also disqualified persons because they are "member[s] of the [disqualified person's] family." This results because the term *members of the family* includes spouses, as well as "brothers and sisters (whether by the whole or half blood) and their spouses." Thus, 100 percent of the profits interest of the partnership is owned by disqualified persons, thereby making the partnership a disqualified person.

The agent determined that the partnership (through its four partners) will be responsible for paying a 25 percent tax on the excess benefit (that is, the $200,000 per year in annual excessive rent it received) and must also give the museum back the $200,000 per year in excess rent for each year under audit. If the partnership does not pay the tax and undo the transaction by the end of the taxable period, it will face an additional tax equal to 200 percent of the excess benefit involved. Thus, the partnership could have total liability in this matter of $50,000 in tax for each year, plus $200,000 per year which must be repaid to the museum to undo the transaction. If this is not paid in a timely fashion, a 200 percent tax (equal to $400,000 for each year) could be facing the partners.

Unlike Jack Dunlop, Betty's request to abate the excise tax in her case was denied. The IRS agent determined that the board of directors could have easily verified the true rental value of the property by merely contacting any number of reputable commercial real estate brokers in the area. However, they chose instead to enter into the transaction expeditiously, and they blindly presumed that any friends of Betty must be friends of the museum. Moreover, Betty never revealed to the board her knowledge that the proposed rental value was too high, even though Betty had spoken to her stepbrother prior to the board's brief deliberations on the lease. Instead, Betty justified in her mind her decision to keep quiet by telling herself that the museum was benefited by the transaction. Unable to establish good cause for the partnership's excessive rental income, Betty and her partners have paid the first-tier excise tax, repaid the museum the excessive rent, and filed for bankruptcy.

Betty's situation also holds an important lesson: Be careful of any arrangement between an applicable tax-exempt organization and any other corporation, partnership, trust, or estate owned to any degree by a disqualified person or such person's spouse, ancestors, children, grandchildren, great grandchildren, brothers, sisters, or the spouses of any of the foregoing. This is a vast range of relatives, and great care is therefore necessary to avoid inadvertently triggering the intermediate sanctions law. In the above situation, the intermediate sanctions excise tax would have applied even if Betty had not owned any portion of the partnership, because members of the disqualified person's family still owned a total of more than a 35 percent profits interest. This problem could have been avoided if the museum's board of directors had obtained relevant rental information so they could determine the fair market value of the property they were renting.

HOWARD McKENZIE AND MARY ADAMS

There is an old saying, "Ignorance is bliss." That saying aptly fits the last two individuals introduced in the Prologue. Howard McKenzie, the proud president of a small private college, is paid $250,000 per year, making him the second highest paid administrative person (behind the football coach). Mary Adams is the equally proud founder and executive director of a fledgling advocacy group, and, at $195,000 per year, the highest paid employee of the organization. Both love their jobs and both brag to friends about their generous salaries and benefits. Unfortunately, because they are both so consumed with the day-to-day duties of their jobs, neither Howard nor Mary has been reading the literature serving the nonprofit community, which is piling up in their in-boxes. Consequently, they have not yet heard the term *intermediate sanctions.*

Howard's and Mary's blissful ignorance of the law is soon to end. Both of their organizations have been selected for audit by the IRS as a result of determinations that Howard and Mary are receiving excessive compensation from their respective organizations. These allegations were filed with the local IRS District Office by disgruntled members of competing tax-exempt organizations. These same disgruntled members have also sent their allegations to the local media.

CONCLUSION

Months or even years will pass before we can judge whether the new intermediate sanctions statute can accomplish its intended purposes or whether it has merely become another subtle trap for the unwary. Given the many nuances and vagaries of this law, one can only hope that the Treasury Department and the IRS will issue detailed guidance expeditiously and that the law will be applied with a liberal amount of common sense so that hard-working and talented individuals are not dissuaded from serving as officers, directors, and employees of nonprofit organizations.

Intermediate Sanctions Law

SEC. 4958. TAXES ON EXCESS BENEFIT TRANSACTIONS.

(a) INITIAL TAXES.—

(1) ON THE DISQUALIFIED PERSON.—There is hereby imposed on each excess benefit transaction a tax equal to 25 percent of the excess benefit. The tax imposed by this paragraph shall be paid by any disqualified person referred to in subsection (f)(1) with respect to such transaction.

(2) ON THE MANAGEMENT.—In any case in which a tax is imposed by paragraph (1), there is hereby imposed on the participation of any organization manager in the excess benefit transaction, knowing that it is such a transaction, a tax equal to 10 percent of the excess benefit, unless such participation is not willful and is due to reasonable cause. The tax imposed by this paragraph shall be paid by any organization manager who participated in the excess benefit transaction.

(b) ADDITIONAL TAX ON THE DISQUALIFIED PERSON.—In any case in which an initial tax is imposed by subsection (a)(1) on an excess benefit transaction and the excess benefit involved in such transaction is not corrected within the taxable period, there is hereby imposed a tax equal to 200 percent of the excess benefit involved. The

117

tax imposed by this subsection shall be paid by any disqualified person referred to in subsection (f)(1) with respect to such transaction.

(c) EXCESS BENEFIT TRANSACTION; EXCESS BENEFIT.—For purposes of this section—

(1) EXCESS BENEFIT TRANSACTION.—

(A) IN GENERAL.—The term "excess benefit transaction" means any transaction in which an economic benefit is provided by an applicable tax-exempt organization directly or indirectly to or for the use of any disqualified person if the value of the economic benefit provided exceeds the value of the consideration (including the performance of services) received for providing such benefit. For purposes of the preceding sentence, an economic benefit shall not be treated as consideration for the performance of services unless such organization clearly indicated its intent to so treat such benefit.

(B) EXCESS BENEFIT.—The term "excess benefit" means the excess referred to in subparagraph (A).

(2) AUTHORITY TO INCLUDE CERTAIN OTHER PRIVATE INUREMENT.—To the extent provided in regulations prescribed by the Secretary, the term "excess benefit transaction" includes any transaction in which the amount of any economic benefit provided to or for the use of a disqualified person is determined in whole or in part by the revenues of 1 or more activities of the organization but only if such transaction results in inurement not permitted under paragraph (3) or (4) of section 501(c), as the case may be. In the case of any such transaction, the excess benefit shall be the amount of the inurement not so permitted.

(d) SPECIAL RULES.—For purposes of this section—

(1) JOINT AND SEVERAL LIABILITY.—If more than 1 person is liable for any tax imposed by subsection (a) or subsection (b), all such persons shall be jointly and severally liable for such tax.

(2) LIMIT FOR MANAGEMENT.—With respect to any 1 excess benefit transaction, the maximum amount of the tax imposed by subsection (a)(2) shall not exceed $10,000.

(e) APPLICABLE TAX-EXEMPT ORGANIZATION.—For purposes of this subchapter, the term "applicable tax-exempt organization" means—

(1) any organization which (without regard to any excess benefit) would be described in paragraph (3) or (4) of section 501(c) and exempt from tax under section 501(a), and

(2) any organization which was described in paragraph (1) at any time during the 5-year period ending on the date of the transaction.

Such term shall not include a private foundation (as defined in section 509(a)).

(f) OTHER DEFINITIONS.—For purposes of this section—

(1) DISQUALIFIED PERSON.—The term "disqualified person" means, with respect to any transaction—

(A) any person who was, at any time during the 5-year period ending on the date of such transaction, in a position to exercise substantial influence over the affairs of the organization,

(B) a member of the family of an individual described in subparagraph (A), and

(C) a 35-percent controlled entity.

(2) ORGANIZATION MANAGER.—The term "organization manager" means, with respect to any applicable tax-exempt organization, any officer, director, or trustee of such organization (or any individual having powers or responsibilities similar to those of officers, directors, or trustees of the organization).

(3) 35-PERCENT CONTROLLED ENTITY.—

(A) IN GENERAL.—The term "35-percent controlled entity" means—

(i) a corporation in which persons described in subparagraph (A) or (B) of paragraph (1) own more than 35 percent of the total combined voting power,

(ii) a partnership in which such persons own more than 35 percent of the profits interest, and

(iii) a trust or estate in which such persons own more than 35 percent of the beneficial interest.

(B) CONSTRUCTIVE OWNERSHIP RULES.—Rules similar to the rules of paragraphs (3) and (4) of section 4946(a) shall apply for purposes of this paragraph.

(4) FAMILY MEMBERS.—The members of an individual's family shall be determined under section 4946(d); except that such members also shall include the brothers and sisters (whether by the whole or half blood) of the individual and their spouses.

(5) TAXABLE PERIOD.—The term "taxable period" means, with respect to any excess benefit transaction, the period beginning

with the date on which the transaction occurs and ending on the earliest of—

(A) the date of mailing a notice of deficiency under section 6212 with respect to the tax imposed by subsection (a)(1), or

(B) the date on which the tax imposed by subsection (a)(1) is assessed.

(6) CORRECTION.—The terms "correction" and "correct" mean, with respect to any excess benefit transaction, undoing the excess benefit to the extent possible, and taking any additional measures necessary to place the organization in a financial position not worse than that in which it would be if the disqualified person were dealing under the highest fiduciary standards.

(b) APPLICATION OF PRIVATE INUREMENT RULE TO TAX-EXEMPT ORGANIZATIONS DESCRIBED IN SECTION 501(c)(4).—

(1) IN GENERAL.—Paragraph (4) of section 501(c) is amended by inserting "(A)" after "(4)" and by adding at the end the following:

"(B) Subparagraph (A) shall not apply to an entity unless no part of the net earnings of such entity inures to the benefit of any private shareholder or individual."

(2) SPECIAL RULE FOR CERTAIN COOPERATIVES.—In the case of an organization operating on a cooperative basis which, before the date of the enactment of this Act, was determined by the Secretary of the Treasury or his delegate, to be described in section 501(c)(4) of the Internal Revenue Code of 1986 and exempt from tax under section 501(a) of such Code, the allocation or return of net margins or capital to the members of such organization in accordance with its incorporating statute and bylaws shall not be treated for purposes of such Code as the inurement of the net earnings of such organization to the benefit of any private shareholder or individual. The preceding sentence shall apply only if such statute and bylaws are substantially as such statute and bylaws were in existence on the date of the enactment of this Act.

(c) TECHNICAL AND CONFORMING AMENDMENTS.—

(1) Subsection (e) of section 4955 is amended—

(A) by striking "SECTION 4945" in the heading and inserting "SECTIONS 4945 AND 4958", and

(B) by inserting before the period "or an excess benefit for purposes of section 4958".

(2) Subsections (a), (b), and (c) of section 4963 are each amended by inserting "4958," after "4955,".

(3) Subsection (e) of section 6213 is amended by inserting "4958 (relating to private excess benefit)," before "4971".

(4) Paragraphs (2) and (3) of section 7422(g) are each amended by inserting "4958," after "4955,".

(5) Subsection (b) of section 7454 is amended by inserting "or whether an organization manager (as defined in section 4958(f)(2)) has 'knowingly' participated in an excess benefit transaction (as defined in section 4958(c))," after "section 4912(b),".

(6) The table of subchapters for chapter 42 is amended by striking the last item and inserting the following:

"SUBCHAPTER D. Failure by certain charitable organizations to meet certain qualification requirements.

"SUBCHAPTER E. Abatement of first and second tier taxes in certain cases.".

(d) EFFECTIVE DATES.—

(1) IN GENERAL.—The amendments made by this section (other than subsection (b)) shall apply to excess benefit transactions occurring on or after September 14, 1995.

(2) BINDING CONTRACTS.—The amendments referred to in paragraph (1) shall not apply to any benefit arising from a transaction pursuant to any written contract which was binding on September 13, 1995, and at all times thereafter before such transaction occurred.

(3) APPLICATION OF PRIVATE INUREMENT RULE TO TAX-EXEMPT ORGANIZATIONS DESCRIBED IN SECTION 501(c)(4).—

(A) IN GENERAL.—The amendment made by subsection (b) shall apply to inurement occurring on or after September 14, 1995.

(B) BINDING CONTRACTS.—The amendment made by subsection (b) shall not apply to any inurement occurring before January 1, 1997, pursuant to a written contract which was binding on September 13, 1995, and at all times thereafter before such inurement occurred.

SEC. 1312. REPORTING OF CERTAIN EXCISE TAXES AND OTHER INFORMATION.

(a) REPORTING BY ORGANIZATIONS DESCRIBED IN SECTION 501(c)(3).—Subsection (b) of section 6033 (relating to certain organizations described in section 501(c)(3)) is amended by striking "and" at the end of paragraph (9), by redesignating paragraph (10) as paragraph (14), and by inserting after paragraph (9) the following new paragraphs:

"(10) the respective amounts (if any) of the taxes paid by the organization during the taxable year under the following provisions:

"(A) section 4911 (relating to tax on excess expenditures to influence legislation),

"(B) section 4912 (relating to tax on disqualifying lobbying expenditures of certain organizations), and

"(C) section 4955 (relating to taxes on political expenditures of section 501(c)(3) organizations),

"(11) the respective amounts (if any) of the taxes paid by the organization, or any disqualified person with respect to such organization, during the taxable year under section 4958 (relating to taxes on private excess benefit from certain charitable organizations),

"(12) such information as the Secretary may require with respect to any excess benefit transaction (as defined in section 4958),

"(13) such information with respect to disqualified persons as the Secretary may prescribe, and".

(b) ORGANIZATIONS DESCRIBED IN SECTION 501(c)(4).—Section 6033 is amended by redesignating subsection (f) as subsection (g) and by inserting after subsection (e) the following new subsection:

"(f) CERTAIN ORGANIZATIONS DESCRIBED IN SECTION 501(c)(4).—Every organization described in section 501(c)(4) which is subject to the requirements of subsection (a) shall include on the return required under subsection (a) the information referred to in paragraphs (11), (12) and (13) of subsection (b) with respect to such organization.".

(c) EFFECTIVE DATE.—The amendments made by this section shall apply to returns for taxable years beginning after the date of the enactment of this Act.

SEC. 1313. EXEMPT ORGANIZATIONS REQUIRED TO PROVIDE COPY OF RETURN.

(a) REQUIREMENT TO PROVIDE COPY.—

(1) Subparagraph (A) of section 6104(e)(1) (relating to public inspection of annual returns) is amended to read as follows:

"(A) IN GENERAL.—During the 3-year period beginning on the filing date—

"(i) a copy of the annual return filed under section 6033 (relating to returns by exempt organizations) by any organization to which this paragraph applies shall be made available by such organization for inspection during regular business hours by any individual at the principal office of such organization and, if such organization regularly maintains 1 or more regional or district offices having 3 or more employees, at each such regional or district office, and

"(ii) upon request of an individual made at such principal office or such a regional or district office, a copy of such annual return shall be provided to such individual without charge other than a reasonable fee for any reproduction and mailing costs.

The request described in clause (ii) must be made in person or in writing. If the request under clause (ii) is made in person, such copy shall be provided immediately and, if made in writing, shall be provided within 30 days.".

(2) Clause (ii) of section 6104(e)(2)(A) is amended by inserting before the period at the end the following: "(and, upon request of an individual made at such principal office or such a regional or district office, a copy of the material requested to be available for inspection under this subparagraph shall be provided (in accordance with the last sentence of paragraph (1)(A)) to such individual without charge other than reasonable fee for any reproduction and mailing costs)".

(3) Subsection (e) of section 6104 is amended by adding at the end the following new paragraph:

"(3) LIMITATION.—Paragraph (1)(A)(ii) (and the corresponding provision of paragraph (2)) shall not apply to any request if, in accordance with regulations promulgated by the Secretary, the organization has made the requested documents widely available, or, the Secretary determines, upon application by an organization, that such request is part of a harassment campaign and that compliance with such request is not in the public interest.".

(b) INCREASE IN PENALTY FOR WILLFUL FAILURE TO ALLOW PUBLIC INSPECTION OF CERTAIN RETURNS, ETC.—Section 6685 is amended by striking "$1,000" and inserting "$5,000".

(c) EFFECTIVE DATE.—The amendments made by this section shall apply to requests made on or after the 60th day after the Secretary of the Treasury first issues the regulations referred to section 6104(e)(3) of the Internal Revenue Code of 1986 (as added by subsection (a)(3)).

SEC. 1314. INCREASE IN PENALTIES ON EXEMPT ORGANIZA-
TIONS FOR FAILURE TO FILE COMPLETE AND TIMELY ANNUAL
RETURNS.

(a) IN GENERAL.—Subparagraph (A) of section 6652(c)(1) (relating to annual returns under section 6033) is amended by striking
"$10" and inserting "$20" and by striking "$5,000" and inserting
"$10,000".

(b) LARGER PENALTY ON ORGANIZATIONS HAVING
GROSS RECEIPTS IN EXCESS OF $1,000,000.—Subparagraph (A) of
section 6652(c)(1) is amended by adding at the end the following
new sentence: "In the case of an organization having gross receipts
exceeding $1,000,000 for any year, with respect to the return re-
quired under section 6033 for such year, the first sentence of this
subparagraph shall be applied by substituting '$100' for '$20' and, in
lieu of applying the second sentence of this subparagraph, the maximum penalty under this subparagraph shall not exceed $50,000.".

(c) EFFECTIVE DATE.—The amendments made by this section
shall apply to returns for taxable years ending on or after the date of
the enactment of this Act.

Intermediate Sanctions Legislative History

INTERMEDIATE SANCTIONS FOR EXCESS BENEFIT TRANSACTIONS

The bill imposes penalty excise taxes as an intermediate sanction in cases where organizations exempt from tax under section 501(c)(3) or 501(c)(4) (other than private foundations, which are subject to a separate penalty regime under current law) engage in an "excess benefit transaction." In such cases, intermediate sanctions may be imposed on certain disqualified persons (i.e., insiders) who improperly benefit from an excess benefit transaction and on organization managers who participate in such a transaction knowing that it is improper.

An "excess benefit transaction" is defined as: (1) any transaction in which an economic benefit is provided to, or for the use of, any disqualified person if the value of the economic benefit provided directly by the organization (or indirectly through a controlled entity[1]) to such person exceeds the value of consideration (including performance of services) received by the organization for providing such benefit; and (2) to the extent provided in Treasury Department regulations, any transaction in which the amount of any economic benefit provided to, or for the use of, any disqualified person is determined in whole or in part by the revenues of the organization, provided that the transaction constitutes prohibited inurement under present-law section 501(c)(3) or under section 501(c)(4), as amended. Thus, "excess benefit transactions" subject to excise taxes include transactions in which a disqualified person engages in a nonfair-market-value transaction with an organization or receives unreasonable compensation, as well as financial arrangements (to the extent provided in Treasury regulations) under which a disqualified person receives payment based on the organization's income in a transaction that violates the present-law private inurement prohibition. The Treasury Department is instructed to issue prompt guidance providing examples of revenue-sharing arrangements that violate the private inurement prohibition; such guidance shall be applicable on a prospective basis.[2]

Existing tax-law standards (see sec. 162) apply in determining reasonableness of compensation and fair market value.[3] In applying such standards, the Committee intends that the parties to a transaction are entitled to rely on a rebuttable presumption of reasonableness with respect to a compensation arrangement with a disqualified person if such arrangement was approved by a board of directors or trustees (or committee thereof) that: (1) was composed entirely of individuals unrelated to and not subject to the control of the disqualified person(s) involved in the arrangement;[4] (2) obtained and relied upon appropriate data as to comparability (e.g., compensation levels paid by similarly situated organizations, both taxable and tax-exempt, for functionally comparable positions; the location of the organization, including the availability of similar specialties in the geographic area; independent compensation surveys by nationally recognized independent firms; or actual written offers from similar institutions competing for the services of the disqualified person); and (3) adequately documented the basis for its determination (e.g., the record includes an evaluation of the individual whose compensation was being established and the basis for determining that the individual's compensation was reasonable in light of that evaluation and data).[5] If these three criteria are satisfied, penalty excise taxes could be imposed under the proposal only if the IRS develops sufficient contrary evidence to rebut the probative value of the evidence put forth by the parties to the transaction (e.g., the IRS could establish that the compensation data relied upon by the parties was not for functionally comparable positions or that the disqualified person, in fact, did not substantially perform the responsibilities of such position). A similar rebuttable presumption would arise with respect to the reasonableness of the valuation of property sold or otherwise transferred (or purchased) by an organization to (or from) a disqualified person if the sale or transfer (or purchase) is approved by an independent board that uses appropriate comparability data and adequately documents its determination. The Secretary of the Treasury and IRS are instructed to issue guidance in connection with the reasonableness standard that incorporates this presumption.

The bill specifically provides that the payment of personal expenses and benefits to or for the benefit of disqualified persons, and nonfair-market-value transactions benefiting such persons, would be treated as compensation only if it is clear that the organization intended and made the payments as compensation for services. In determining whether such payments or transactions are, in fact, compensation, the relevant factors include whether the appropriate decision-making body approved the transfer as compensation in accordance with established procedures and whether the organization and the recipient reported the transfer (except in the case of nontaxable fringe benefits) as compensation on the relevant forms (i.e., the organization's Form 990, the Form W-2 or Form 1099 provided by the organization to the recipient, the recipient's Form 1040, and other required returns).[6]

Consistent with the rule that payment of personal expenses and benefits to or for the benefit of disqualified persons and nonfair-market-value transactions benefiting such persons are treated as compensation only if it is clear that the organization intended and made the payments as compensation for services, any reimbursements by the organization of excise tax liability are treated as an excess benefit unless they are included in the disqualified person's compensation during the year the reimbursement is made. The total compensation package, including the amount of any reimbursement, is subject to the reasonableness requirement. Similarly, the payment by an applicable tax-exempt organization of premiums for an insurance policy providing liability insurance to a disqualified person for excess benefit taxes is an excess benefit transaction unless such premiums are treated as part of the compensation paid to such disqualified person.[7]

"Disqualified person" means any individual who is in a position to exercise substantial influence over the affairs of the organization, whether by virtue of being an organization manager or otherwise.[8] In addition, "disqualified persons" include certain family members and 35-percent owned entities[9] of a disqualified person, as well as any person who was a disqualified person at any time during the five-year period prior to the transaction at issue. A person having the title of "officer, director, or trustee" does not automatically have the status of a disqualified person.[10] In addition, the Secretary of Treasury has authority to promulgate rules exempting broad categories of individuals from the category of "disqualified persons" (e.g., full-time bona fide employees who receive economic benefits of less than a threshold amount or persons who have taken a vow of poverty).

A disqualified person who benefits from an excess benefit transaction is subject to a first-tier penalty tax equal to 25 percent of the amount of the excess benefit (i.e., the amount by which a transaction differs from fair market value, the amount of compensation exceeding reasonable compensation, or (under Treasury regulations) the amount of a prohibited transaction based on the organization's gross or net income). Organization managers who participate in an excess benefit transaction knowing that it is an improper transaction are subject to a first-tier penalty tax of 10 percent of the amount of the excess benefit (subject to a maximum penalty of $10,000).[11]

Additional, second-tier taxes may be imposed on a disqualified person if there is no correction of the excess benefit transaction within a specified time period.[12] In such cases, the disqualified person is subject to a penalty tax equal to 200 percent of the amount of excess benefit. For this purpose, the term "correction" means undoing the excess benefit to the extent possible and taking any additional measures necessary to place the organization in a financial position not worse than that in which it would be if the disqualified person were dealing under the highest fiduciary standards.

The intermediate sanctions for "excess benefit transactions" may be imposed by the IRS in lieu of (or in addition to) revocation of an organization's tax-exempt status.[13] If more than one disqualified person or manager is liable for a penalty excise tax, than all such persons are jointly and severally liable for such tax. As under current law, a three-year statute of limitations applies, except in the case of fraud (sec. 6501). Under the bill, the IRS has authority to abate the excise tax penalty (under present-law section 4962) if it is established that the violation was due to reasonable cause and not due to willful neglect and the transaction at issue was corrected within the specified period.

To prevent avoidance of the penalty excise taxes in cases of private inurement of assets of a previously tax-exempt organization, the bill provides that an organization will be treated as an applicable tax-exempt organization subject to the excise taxes on excess benefit transactions if, at any time during the 5-year period preceding the transaction, it was a tax-exempt organization described in section 501(c)(3) or 501(c)(4), or a successor to such an organization.

Effective date.—The provision generally applies to excess benefit transactions occurring on or after September 14, 1995. The provision does not apply, however, to any benefits arising out of a transaction pursuant to a written contract which was binding on September 13, 1995, and at all times thereafter before such benefits arose, and the terms of which have not materially changed.

In addition, the Committee intends that parties to transactions entered into after September 13, 1995, and before January 1, 1997, are entitled to rely on the rebuttable presumption of reasonableness if, within a reasonable period (e.g., 90 days) after entering into the compensation package, the parties satisfy the three criteria that give rise to the presumption. After December 31, 1996, the rebuttable presumption should arise only if the three criteria are satisfied prior to payment of the compensation (or, to the extent provided by the Secretary of the Treasury, within a reasonable period thereafter).

ADDITIONAL FILING AND PUBLIC DISCLOSURE RULES

Reporting of information with respect to certain disqualified persons, excise tax penalties and excess benefit transactions.—Tax-exempt organizations are required to disclose on their Form 990 such information with respect to disqualified persons as the Secretary of the Treasury may prescribe. The Committee intends that this requirement is not intended to limit the Secretary's authority under section 6033(a)(1) to require information on annual returns filed by exempt organizations for the purpose of carrying out the internal revenue laws. In addition, exempt organizations are required to disclose on their Form 990 such information as the Secretary of the Treasury may require with respect to "excess benefit transactions" (described above) and any other excise tax penalties paid during the year under present-law sections 4911 (excess lobbying expenditures), 4912 (disqualifying lobbying expenditures), or 4955 (political expenditures), including the amount of the excise tax penalties paid with respect to such transactions, the nature of the activity, and the parties involved.[14]

Furnishing copies of documents.—The bill also provides that a tax-exempt organization that is subject to the public inspection rules of present-law section 6104(e)(1) (i.e., any tax-exempt organization, other than a private foundation, that files a Form 990) is required to comply with requests made in writing or in person from individuals who seek a copy of the organization's Form 990 or the organization's application for recognition of tax-exempt status and certain related documents. Upon such a request, the organization is required to supply copies without charge other than a reasonable fee for reproduction and mailing costs. If so requested, copies must be supplied of the Forms 990 for any of the organization's three most recent taxable years. If the request for copies is made in person, then the organization must immediately provide such copies. If the request for copies is made in writing, then copies must be provided within 30 days. However, an organization may be relieved of its obligation to provide copies if, in accordance with regulations to be promulgated by the Secretary of the Treasury, (1) the organization has made the requested documents widely available or (2) the Secretary of the Treasury determined, upon application by the organization, that the organization was subject to a harassment campaign such that a waiver of the obligation to provide copies would be in the public interest.

Penalties for failure to file timely or complete return.—The section 6652(c)(1)(A) penalty imposed on a tax-exempt organization that either fails to file a Form 990 in a timely manner or fails to include all required information on a Form 990 is increased from the present-law level of $10 for each day the failure continues (with a maximum penalty with respect to any one return of the lesser of $5,000 or five percent of the organization's gross receipts) to $20 for each day the failure continues (with a maximum penalty with respect to any one return of the lesser of $10,000 or five percent of the organization's gross receipts). Under the bill, organizations with annual gross receipts exceeding $1 million are subject to a penalty under section 6652(c)(1)(A) of $100 for each day the failure continues (with a maximum penalty with respect to any one return of $50,000). As under present law, no penalty may be imposed under section 6652(c)(1)(A) if it were shown that the failure to file a complete return was due to reasonable cause (sec. 6652(c)(3)).

Penalties for failure to allow public inspection or provide copies.—The section 6652(c)(1)(C) penalty imposed on tax-exempt organizations that fail to allow public inspection or provide copies of certain annual returns or applications for exemption is increased from the present-law level of $10 per day (with a maximum of $5,000) to $20 per day (with a maximum of $10,000). In addition, the section 6685 penalty for willful failure to allow public inspections or provide copies is increased from the present-law level of $1,000 to $5,000.

Effective date.—The public inspection provisions governing tax-exempt organizations generally apply to requests made no earlier than 60 days after the date on which the Treasury Department publishes the anti-harassment regulations required under the provisions. However, the Committee expects that organizations will comply voluntarily with the public inspection provisions prior to the issuance of such regulations. The provisions regarding the reporting on annual returns of excise tax penalties and excess benefit transactions are effective for returns with respect to taxable years beginning on or after the date of enactment.

NOTES

1. A tax-exempt organization cannot avoid the private inurement proscription by causing a controlled entity to engage in an excess benefit

transaction. Thus, for example, if a tax-exempt organization causes its taxable subsidiary to pay excessive compensation to an individual who is a disqualified person with respect to the parent organization, such transaction would be an excess benefit transaction.

2. Under present law, certain revenue sharing arrangements have been determined not to constitute private inurement (see e.g., GCM 38283; GCM 38905; and GCM 39674) and, under the proposal, it would continue to be the case that not all revenue sharing arrangements would be improper private inurement. However, the Committee intends no inference that Treasury or the Internal Revenue Service are bound by any particular prior unpublished rulings in this area.

3. In this regard, the Committee intends that an individual need not necessarily accept reduced compensation merely because he or she renders services to a tax-exempt, as opposed to a taxable, organization. Cf. Treas. Reg. sec. 53.4941(d)-3(c)(1).

4. A reciprocal approval arrangement whereby an individual approves compensation of the disqualified person, and the disqualified person, in turn, approves the individual's compensation does not satisfy the independence requirement.

5. The fact that a State or local legislative or agency body may have authorized or approved of a particular compensation package paid to a disqualified person is not determinative of the reasonableness of compensation paid for purposes of the excise tax penalties provided for by the proposal. Similarly, such authorization or approval is not determinative of whether a revenue sharing arrangement violates the private inurement proscription.

6. With the exception of nontaxable fringe benefits described in present-law section 132 and other types of nontaxable transfers such as employer-provided health benefits and contributions to qualified pension plans, an organization cannot demonstrate at the time of an IRS audit that it clearly indicated its intent to treat economic benefits provided to a disqualified person as compensation for services merely by claiming that such benefits may be viewed as part of the disqualified person's total compensation package. Rather, the organization would be required to provide substantiation that is contemporaneous with the transfer of economic benefits at issue.

7. In addition, because individuals may be both members of, and disqualified persons with respect to, a non-exclusive applicable tax-exempt organization (e.g., a museum or neighborhood civic organization) and receive certain benefits (e.g., free admission, discounted gift shop purchases) in their capacity as members (rather than in their capacity as disqualified persons), the Committee expects that the Treasury Department will provide guidance clarifying that such membership benefits may be excluded from consideration under the private inurement proscription and intermediate sanction rules.

8. Under the bill, a person could be in a position to exercise substantial influence over a tax-exempt organization despite the fact that such person is not an employee of (and receives no compensation directly from) a tax-exempt organization, but is formally an employee of (and is directly compensated by) a subsidiary—even a taxable subsidiary—controlled by the parent tax-exempt organization.

9. Family members are determined under present-law section 4946(d), except that such members also would include siblings (whether by whole or half blood) of the individual, and spouses of such siblings. "35-percent owned entities" mean corporations in which disqualified persons own stock possessing more than 35 percent of the combined voting power, as well as partnerships and trusts or estates in which disqualified persons own more than 35 percent of the profits interest or beneficial interest. As under present-law section 4946(a), the term "combined voting power" includes voting power represented by holdings of voting stock, actual or constructive, but does not include voting rights held only as a director or trustee. See Treas. Reg. sec. 53.4946-1(a)(5).

10. The IRS has issued a general counsel memorandum indicating that all physicians are considered "insiders" for purposes of applying the private inurement proscription. The Committee intends that physicians will be disqualified persons only if they are in a position to exercise substantial influence over the affairs of an organization.

11. In determining who is an organization manager, the Committee intends that principles similar to those set forth in regulations issued under sections 4946 and 4955 with respect to final authority or responsibility for an expenditure be applied. (See Treas. Reg. secs. 53.4946-1(f)(1)(ii), 53.4946-1(f)(2), 53.4955-1(b)(2)(ii)(B), and 53.4955-1(b)(2)(iii).)

12. Correction must be made on or prior to the earlier of (1) the date of mailing of a notice of deficiency under section 6212 with respect to the first-tier penalty excise tax imposed on the disqualified person, or (2) the date on which such tax is assessed.

13. In general, the intermediate sanctions are the sole sanction imposed in those cases in which the excess benefit does not rise to a level where it calls into question whether, on the whole, the organization functions as a charitable or other tax-exempt organization. In practice, revocation of tax-exempt status, with or without the imposition of excise taxes, would occur only when the organization no longer operates as a charitable organization.

14. The penalties applicable to failure to file a timely, complete, and accurate return apply for failure to comply with these requirements. In addition, the Committee intends that the IRS implement its plan to require additional Form 990 reporting regarding (1) changes to the governing board or the certified accounting firm, (2) such information as the Treasury Secretary may require relating to professional fundraising fees paid by the organization, and (3) aggregate payments (by related entities) in excess of $100,000 to the highest-paid employees.

APPENDIX C

The History of Intermediate Sanctions

The rules creating intermediate sanctions, as enacted by Congress and signed into law by the President on July 30, 1996 (P.L. 104-168, 104th Cong., 2d Sess. (1996)), have an extensive and convoluted history.

This body of law is essentially the same as that contained in the Revenue Reconciliation Act of 1995, which passed Congress late in 1995 (H.R. 2491, 104th Cong., 1st Sess. (1995)). However, this Act was vetoed by the President as part of the legislative branch-executive branch battle over the reach of federal budget legislation for fiscal year 1996.

It was thought by many that intermediate sanctions would be enacted as part of subsequent budget and tax legislation. This view turned out to be erroneous, inasmuch as intermediate sanctions came into being as the consequence of enactment of the Taxpayer Bill of Rights 2. Indeed, the sanctions were included as part of that legislation to generate revenue in support of other of its provisions.

PRIVATE FOUNDATION ORIGINS

The format of—as well as the spirit underlying—intermediate sanctions can be traced back more than 30 years. Motivated in large part by a report from the Department of the Treasury in 1965, Congress by the close of the 1960s was in the process of cracking down on the activities of private foundations. As part of that effort, it conjured up rules much like those imposing the new intermediate sanctions. These rules, adopted as a significant portion of the Tax Reform Act of 1969, are in the Internal Revenue Code as Sections 4941–4948. This body of law imposes several taxes on disqualified persons who engage in what is deemed inappropriate behavior with private foundations.

The provision bearing the closest proximity to intermediate sanctions is Section 4941, which contains prohibitions on self-dealing transactions between private foundations and disqualified persons. This body of law identifies six types of transactions that generally constitute prohibited self-dealing:

1. A sale, exchange, or leasing of property between a private foundation and a disqualified person;
2. The lending of money or other extension of credit between a private foundation and a disqualified person;
3. The furnishing of goods, services, or facilities between a private foundation and a disqualified person;
4. The payment of compensation (or payment or reimbursement of expenses, unless reasonable) by a private foundation to a disqualified person;
5. A transfer to, or use by or for the benefit of, a disqualified person of the income or assets of a private foundation; and
6. An agreement by a private foundation to make any payment of money or other property to a government official, other than certain arrangements for employment after government service.

Once these rules were added to the Internal Revenue Code, the push began to craft a comparable body of law for public charities. For years that effort was unsuccessful because public charities were not perceived as involved in the same problem areas as private foundations. Over time, that attitude changed. In Congress, at the IRS, and in other tax policy circles, the thinking about the activities of public charities in the mid-1990s was as negative as was the thinking about private foundations in those circles in the mid-1960s. Intermediate sanctions are a direct product of the law created by the 1969 Act; it just took a quarter of a century to get here.

HOUSE OVERSIGHT SUBCOMMITTEE IN THE 1980s

The first occasion Congress had to create a system of taxes on public charities for certain expenditures arose on enactment of the Tax Reform

Act of 1976, when a tax on excess lobbying expenditures was formulated (Internal Revenue Code Section 4911). In several respects, however, this tax, was not like the private foundation tax approach. For example, this tax regime does not tax any organization managers—trustees, directors, officers, and key employees—who caused the charitable organization to make the expenditure, knowing it was an inappropriate outlay.

Seeds of today's intermediate sanctions law were planted in the fertile ground of the House Subcommittee on Oversight during the 1980s. That subcommittee of the House Committee on Ways and Means, then under the chairmanship of Rep. J.J. ("Jake") Pickle (D-Tex.), aggressively reviewed the activities of public charities and other tax-exempt organizations. Among the products of this effort (which included eight days of hearings during 1987) was legislation made part of the Tax Reform Act of 1987, which imposed penalties on public charities for excessive lobbying and also penalized those (usually, directors and officers) who knowingly caused the charities to engage in the lobbying (Internal Revenue Code Section 4912). Tax penalties were also created to tax political campaign expenditures (Section 4955); these rules also tax organization managers. These penalties, particularly the ones for lobbying, represented the first time that Congress had enacted private foundation-type penalties in the realm of public charities.

These penalties launched two trends that affected regulation of the affairs of tax-exempt organizations. One was toward greater reliance on excise taxes and civil penalties (rather than loss of tax-exempt status) as sanctions. The other was a greater willingness to apply taxes and penalties to the individuals involved.

In 1988, the Subcommittee held hearings to review the structure, application, fairness, and effectiveness of the federal civil penalty provisions. In testimony on tax penalties as they apply to tax-exempt organizations, it was suggested that there be a penalty system underlying the private inurement rules, along the lines of those created in the lobbying and political campaign activities context.

In anticipation of these hearings, the IRS, in late 1987, had established a task force to study federal tax penalties. This body—the IRS Commissioner's Executive Task Force on Civil Penalties—issued its recommendations early in 1989. The task force focused on the matter of management of funds of public charities, observing that, for these organizations, "the only sanction for financial abuse of the exemption is termination of exempt status." This forces the tax law enforcer to, in the language of the report, "either impose a very harsh penalty or none at all." The report also observed that the "indefinite nature of the substantive rules governing exempt status makes this remedy [revocation of exemption] of doubtful utility except in major abuse situations." It concluded: "The Service could more effectively enforce charitable standards upon public charities if excise tax penalties similar to those currently applicable to private foundations were extended to some or all public charities."

IMPACT OF HEALTH CARE REFORM EFFORTS

Nothing came of these efforts until about three years later, when the debate over restructuring the nation's health care delivery system heated up. In that setting, legislation was introduced in the House of Representatives in 1991 to tax, by means of excise tax penalties, certain transfers between tax-exempt health care facilities and their board members and other managers (H.R. 4042, 103d Cong., 1st Sess. (1991)). The bill would have brought law authorizing assessments of penalty excise taxes in cases where a medical service organization sells, exchanges, or leases a medical asset to individuals who are disqualified persons with respect to it. The sponsor, Rep. Fortney ("Pete") Stark (D-Cal.), explained that he wanted to discourage boards of tax-exempt health care facilities from selling the facilities to disqualified persons at less than fair market value (137 *Cong. Rec.* E4183 (Nov. 26, 1991)).

Congressman Stark was motivated to initiate this legislation in part because of a hearing held on criteria for tax exemption of nonprofit hospitals ("Tax-Exempt Status of Hospitals, and Establishment of Charity Care Standards," Hearing before the House Committee on Ways and Means, 102d Cong., 1st Sess. (1996)). During the course of that hearing, the then-Commissioner of Internal Revenue, John E. Burke, stated that "agents are reluctant to propose revocation of exemption because the sanction of revocation of a hospital's exempt status greatly outweighs the private gain of a few individuals" (*id.* at 112).

Thus, Rep. Stark proposed a sanction applicable to responsible persons of a tax-exempt health care facility that discourages private inurement without penalizing the hospital. This legislative proposal was formulated on the approach of the private foundation self-dealing rules (see above).

FOCUS ON PUBLIC CHARITY ABUSE

The contemporary intermediate sanctions movement is traceable to a series of hearings, before the House Subcommittee on Oversight, to review the activities of public charities. The first of these hearings took place on June 15, 1993 ("Federal Tax Laws Applicable to the Activities of Tax-Exempt Charitable Organizations," 103d Cong., 1st Sess. (1993)). A focus of the hearings was on the adequacy of then-existing law in relation to instances of private inurement and private benefit.

In an opening statement, Subcommittee Chairman Pickle observed that "some charitable organizations have abused the public trust and have allowed tax-deductible contributions to inure to the benefit of select privileged insiders." He said that staff review of the annual information returns for the 250 largest tax-exempt organizations found that, of the top 2,000 executives at these organizations, 15 percent were paid more than $200,000 per year and 38 of them were paid more than $400,000. He asked:

- "Is it appropriate for a charitable organization to shift five million tax-deductible dollars to its for-profit subsidiary?"
- "[S]hould a medical school vice president be allowed to borrow a million dollars, interest-free, to buy and renovate his house?"
- "[S]hould charitable contributions be used to pay a million dollar salary to the chairman of an educational organization?"
- "[S]hould the administrator of a small pension plan be paid $500,000 in salary?"

He also noted the use of "tax-deductible donations" to provide "charity officials" with "extravagant perks, like luxury cars, servants, chauffeurs, country-club memberships, and extremely lucrative severance packages."

Chairman Pickle said that the purpose of the hearings was to learn "what the IRS knows about these activities, or possible abuses, and whether they should be allowed or stopped," "if Federal law is adequate to ensure compliance by public charities and to appropriately punish wrongdoing," and "if the public is currently being provided access to the information necessary for them to make informed judgments about charitable giving." He added that these hearings "are not an attempt to attack the character and good work of public charities in our cities and neighborhoods."

Rep. Pickle signaled two areas of possible law revision: (1) speed up the IRS audits of tax-exempt organization, and (2) impose a penalty, in cases of private inurement or private benefit, other than revocation of tax exemption.

The first witness at this hearing was the Commissioner of Internal Revenue, Margaret Milner Richardson, who was making her first appearance before a House committee. She summarized the law on private inurement and private benefit, and said that these rules "present diffi-culties for effective tax administration." Endorsing the idea of interme-diate sanctions, she added that having as the sole sanction the revocation of tax exemption "makes enforcement of the charitable or-ganization provisions difficult" and that "it would be useful to provide the Service with a sanction short of revocation to address violations of these [private inurement/benefit] standards."

Commissioner Richardson explained current IRS enforcement activ-ities in this area, noting that "media evangelists, hospitals, and univer-sities continue to be special emphasis areas in our examinations." As to abuse in the private inurement/benefit field, she said that, "in par-ticular, we are concerned about potentially excessive compensation." In general, she observed that, "in considering any new sanctions, con-sideration should also be given to the possibility of clarifying the stan-dards for tax exemption." She added: "Changes to Form 990 to enable the public to have greater knowledge of a public charity's operations may be appropriate."

The second round of these hearings was held on August 2, 1993 (see the citation above to the June 1993 hearings). This round focused on the enforcement activities of the IRS, the implications of the private in-urement rules, and the adequacy of existing public disclosure require-ments (with particular emphasis on the annual information return). Rep. Pickle, in his opening remarks, articulated some of the trouble-some cases that had come to the attention of the Subcommittee:

- With the assets from one charitable organization, an executive paid his child's college tuition, leased a luxury car for his wife, had his kitchen remodeled, and rented a vacation house at a beach. The charity permitted him to charge almost $60,000 in personal expenses to the organization's credit card.
- At a tax-exempt hospital, the chief executive officer used charita-ble assets to pay for such personal items as liquor, china, crystal, perfume, and airplane and theater tickets. The hospital also picked up the tab for the CEO's country club charges and catered lunches, which totaled about $20,000.
- A charity paid $200,000 for its executive director's wedding re-ception and tropical island honeymoon. The charity also made a $90,000 down payment for his home and paid for his trip to a health spa.

Mr. Pickle added: "Admittedly, these examples of abuse do not repre-sent what is occurring at all public charities. I believe that the vast majority of charities serve an invaluable public purpose. These examples, however, do illustrate that charities are not immune from abuse by executives more interested in lining their own pockets than in serving the public."

There were two phases to this hearing. The first was a closed executive session where the Subcommittee heard nondisclosable testimony from IRS field agents about enforcement activities, including specific cases involving questionable practices by tax-exempt organizations. In the second part of the hearing, open to the public, the IRS summarized the cases that were the subject of the executive session, and presented testimony regarding the process by which issues involving private inurement and private benefit are analyzed.

Late in 1994, evolving health care policy and intermediate sanctions converged once again. The occasion was a hearing before the Subcommittee on Select Revenue Measures, of the House Ways and Means Committee, on selected tax provisions in the Administration's Health Security Act (H.R. 3600, 103d Cong., 2d Sess. (1994)). The lead-off witness was Maurice Foley, then Deputy Tax Legislative Counsel (Legislation), Department of the Treasury. His testimony focused on several elements, one of which was intermediate sanctions.

The Treasury contended that health care reform was boosting the case for intermediate sanctions—an outcome that presumably was not intended to be confined to health care providers. Mr. Foley noted the Subcommittee on Oversight's hearings on private inurement, held the year before, and a bill recently introduced by Rep. Stark (see below). He also observed that the "significant restructuring of the health care market that is expected to result from health reform might in certain cases present opportunities for insiders to divert to their own benefit the resources of tax-exempt health care providers."

He indicated that Treasury was working with the Ways and Means Committee and its staff "to consider the possibility of new, intermediate sanctions for clear misuses of resources." He concluded: "Intermediate sanctions may be useful, particularly if they are narrowly targeted at clearly abusive transactions of the type that have given rise to concern, such as unreasonable compensation and bargain transfers provided to insiders. Narrowly targeted intermediate sanctions might be more effective deterrents than the potential loss of exemption."

SELF-DEALING LEGISLATION

In his capacity as the then-Chairman of the Subcommittee on Health, of the House Ways and Means Committee, Rep. Stark introduced, on

November 23, 1993, another of the contemporary versions of intermediate sanctions legislation (H.R. 3697, 103d Cong., 1st Sess. (1993)). This legislation would have applied to all public charities and tax-exempt social welfare organizations. Essentially, the bill would have extended the private foundation prohibitions on self-dealing to these exempt entities.

For this purpose, the term *self-dealing* would generally have been defined to mean any direct or indirect (1) transfer, lease, or license of property between the tax-exempt organization and a disqualified person, and (2) lending of money or other extension of credit between the exempt organization and a disqualified person. There would have been some exceptions: the lending of money by a disqualified person to an exempt organization without interest; or a transfer, lease, or license of property in the ordinary course of the person's trade or business, where the transaction is on a basis comparable to those of similar business transactions.

The term *disqualified person* would have embraced directors, trustees, and officers of the tax-exempt organizations, and individuals having powers or responsibilities similar to them. It would have applied to all *organization managers* who served during the five-year period preceding the self-dealing transaction, members of their family, an entity controlled (35 percent) by them, and physicians serving pursuant to an employment or other contractual relationship. A self-dealing transaction would have generated a 5 percent tax of the amount involved, payable by the participating disqualified person(s). An organization manager who knowingly participated in the act of self-dealing would have been subject to a tax of 2.5 percent, absent reasonable cause. In the event of no timely correction, there would have been an additional self-dealing tax of 200 percent and an organization manager tax of 50 percent. A *correction* would be intended to "place the applicable tax-exempt organization in a financial position not worse than that in which it would be if the disqualified person were dealing under the highest fiduciary standards."

There would also have been a 10 percent tax on private inurement transactions, payable by the tax-exempt organization. Under this proposal, a participating organization manager could be subjected to a 2.5 percent tax (absent reasonable cause) and the "beneficiary" of the inurement could be assessed a 5 percent tax on the amount involved. Additional taxes could apply, in the amounts of 100, 50, and 200 percent, respectively. *Taxable inurement* would mean any "direct or indirect inurement of any part of the net earnings of an applicable tax-exempt organization to the benefit of any disqualified person," other than acts of self-dealing. (A statement by Rep. Stark on this proposal is at 139 *Cong. Rec.* E3057.)

INITIAL SANCTIONS PROPOSAL

On March 16, 1994, the House Subcommittee on Oversight held another hearing on the activities of public charities. Once again, the subject of intermediate sanctions was addressed. On that occasion, the Department of the Treasury revealed its plan for a multipenalty structure to be applicable to tax-exempt charitable and social welfare organizations that engage in certain forms of private inurement. The testimony was presented by the then-Assistant Secretary for Tax Policy, Leslie B. Samuels. Mr. Samuels, recalling the two previous hearings on these general subjects, before the Subcommittee on Oversight in 1993, stated that these hearings "provide a solid foundation for the conclusion that carefully targeted reform measures are needed to improve compliance with tax laws by public charities." He reviewed the state of existing law, observing that it "provides no sanction for violations of the standards for tax exemption [for charitable organizations and social welfare organizations] short of revocation of an organization's exemption."

He emphasized that the Treasury "do[es] not believe that the cases of noncompliance are widespread or representative of the charitable community as a whole." Nonetheless, he said, these cases are causing "concern" and they "demonstrate that the system is not working as it should." Consequently, Treasury was of the view that "a proposal for carefully targeted intermediate sanctions is appropriate at this time," and that what is needed is not "sweeping new regulation" of public charities but rather a "measured response."

The proposal consisted of an excise tax on those who participate in certain forms of private inurement, and measures to strengthen the disclosure requirements that are applicable to most tax-exempt organizations. The excise tax would have been the intermediate sanction, based on the legal concept of consideration.

The disclosure rules would, he said, "increase the information regarding tax-exempt organizations available to the public." The overall plan was projected to generate about $65 million in federal revenue over five years.

Treasury proposed a new excise tax that would be "targeted at the types of abuses that have generated concern and would provide a substantial deterrent to these abuses." This excise tax would have applied to any *excess benefit* provided to an *insider* by a nonprofit organization that is tax-exempt by reason of being a public charity or a social welfare organization. However, the new rules would not have applied to private foundations because of the existing excise tax regime applicable to them.

An *excess benefit* would have been defined as the excess of the value of any benefit provided by the organization over the consideration received by the organization in return for the benefit. The consideration received by the organization would include services provided by the insider. The term *insider* would have embraced persons such as trustees, directors, officers, key employees, and substantial contributors. It would also have included members of the family of insiders and entities in which an insider or family members have significant beneficial interests. An excess benefit provided to a former insider would have been subject to tax if the relevant decision-making body of the organization approved the benefit when the recipient was an insider.

The concept thus was that what the organization received from the insider as consideration would set the standard as to what was *reasonable* in the particular context. The amount of the benefit that was provided to the insider in excess of the consideration amount would be the amount that was *excessive*. This tax would have applied to three types of transactions:

1. The payment of unreasonable compensation by an organization to an insider.
2. A nonfair-market-value transfer in which an insider pays the organization inadequate consideration for property transferred, leased, licensed, or loaned by the organization.
3. The payment of excessive consideration by an organization for property transferred, leased, licensed, or loaned by an insider.

One of the reasons the intermediate sanctions proposal was made applicable with respect to tax-exempt social welfare organizations was evolving health care reform, which, according to Mr. Samuels, "could provide greater opportunities for insiders of health care organizations, including health maintenance organizations . . ., to divert to the insiders' own benefit the resources of these organizations." This proposal was based on the idea that the reasonableness of compensation or other consideration is able to be accurately and fairly determined. The Treasury proposal stated that this reasonableness would be ascertained using all of the "facts and circumstances."

As to compensation, the factors determining what is reasonable would have included the nature of the insider's duties, his or her background and experience, the time he or she devotes to the organization, the size of the organization, general and local economic conditions, and the amount paid by similar organizations to those who perform similar services.

The approval of the compensation or transfer by an independent governing body of the organization would have "weigh[ed] in favor of a finding of reasonableness or adequate consideration." Yet, the weight to be given to this factor would have depended on the circumstances. This illustration was offered: "For example, approval by a nominally independent governing body may be given little weight if the governing body is comprised of close friends of the organization's founder and president who routinely endorse proposals made by that person. On the other hand, approval by a governing body would be given greater weight if the governing body is truly independent and has a demonstrated record of taking its fiduciary responsibilities seriously."

Benefits provided to an insider could have been justified as reasonable compensation only if the organization in fact provided the benefits as compensation for services. This determination would, as well, have been made based on all of the facts and circumstances. The relevant facts would include whether the appropriate decision-making body approved the transfer as compensation in accordance with established procedures and whether the organization and the recipient reported the transfer as compensation on the appropriate federal tax forms. If a non-fair-market-value transfer was not made as compensation for services, it would have been subject to the excise tax even if the insider's compensation would have been reasonable had the transfer been compensatory.

If an organization provided an excess benefit to an insider (including related persons), the insider would have been subject to an initial tax of 25 percent of the amount of the excess benefit. The insider would have had the opportunity to repay the excess benefit with appropriate interest within a prescribed period—this technically is a correction. The initial tax would have been waived (or refunded) only if the excess benefit was provided in circumstances involving reasonable cause. If the correction did not timely occur, the insider would have been subject to a second tax, equal to 200 percent of the excess benefit.

Repayment of an excess benefit by an insider would have been deductible only to the extent that the receipt of the excess benefit increased the insider's taxable income for a prior year. Payment of the tax itself would not have given rise to a deduction.

If a trustee, a director, or an officer (collectively, a manager) approved a transaction knowing that it would result in an excess benefit, the manager would have been subject to a tax of 10 percent of the excess benefit, up to a maximum of $10,000. To ensure that the manager bore the economic burden of the tax, any payment or reimbursement by the organization of a tax imposed on a manager would itself have been treated as an excess benefit provided to the manager. Thus, as an insider, the manager would have been subject to the excise tax on the payment or reimbursement.

The excise tax on excess benefits would have been the sole sanction available in cases in which the excess benefit did not rise to a level where it called into question whether the organization truly is a charitable or social welfare entity. However, if an organization provided an excess benefit that was egregious and substantial, the excise tax would have applied and the organization would have been subject to revocation of its tax exemption. (This proposal was intended to deter an insider from avoiding tax by correcting the benefit and then causing the organization to repay the benefit to the insider when the organization is no longer tax-exempt.)

Treasury also proposed a variety of measures to improve the information provided on the annual information return filed by public charities (usually Form 990) and the availability of that information to the public. The proposal would have increased the penalty for failure to file a timely, complete, and accurate return from $10 to $100 a day for organizations with gross receipts in excess of $1 million for the year involved, subject to a maximum of $50,000 for any one return. For other organizations, the penalty would have been increased to $20 a day, with the maximum for any one return limited to the lesser of $10,000 or 5 percent of the gross receipts of the organization for the year.

This proposal would also have required tax-exempt organizations to provide copies of their annual information returns and applications for recognition of tax exemption (and related materials) to any person who requests the documents and pays a reasonable fee to cover photocopying and mailing costs. Regulations would have been promulgated as to reasonable fees. A charitable organization would have been required to include in its fund-raising solicitations a statement regarding the availability of its annual return.

The penalties for violation of these rules would have been increased from $10 to $20 per day. The maximum penalty per return would have been increased from $5,000 to $10,000. Mr. Samuels added: "We intend to develop rules to protect organizations from the burdens of complying with requests for documents made as part of an organized harassment campaign. One approach to this issue would be to apply a limit on the number of requests that the organization would be required to fulfill within a given period."

An organization would have been required to report on its annual information return the amount of taxes paid because of excess and disqualifying lobbying expenses. Also to be reported would have been transactions involving the payment of excess benefits subject to the proposed excise tax, including excess benefits for which the tax was asserted but then waived due to repayment.

Further, this proposal would have required an organization to report on its annual information return changes in the membership of its governing board, as well as a change in the identity of the certified public accounting firm retained by the organization to examine its books and records.

1994 HEALTH CARE BILL

The controversial health care legislation that occupied Congress throughout 1994—the Health Security Act—included a version of the intermediate sanctions proposal (H.R. 3600, 103d Cong., 2d Sess. (1994)). This proposal would have imposed two-tier penalty taxes in cases where a tax-exempt charitable or social welfare organization, that has as its predominant activity the provision of health care services, engaged in a transaction resulting in *taxable inurement*. This type of inurement would have meant any direct or indirect inurement of any part of the net earnings of an organization to the benefit of a disqualified person. Included would have been unreasonable compensation, a nonfair-market-value transaction with the organization, or a payment based on the organization's net income.

Beneficiaries of taxable inurement would have been subject to a first-tier penalty tax equal to 25 percent of the amount of the inurement. The organization would have been subject to a penalty tax of 5 percent. Directors, officers, and physicians who were under contract with the organization and who knowingly participated in the inurement would have been taxed at a 2.5 percent rate. Additional taxes, to be imposed where the inurement was not timely corrected, would have been at rates of 200, 100, and 50 percent, respectively.

The proposal also would have provided for these sanctions in the form of excise tax penalties that could be imposed on exempt health care organizations. These taxes could have been imposed if the organization failed to satisfy one or more of a litany of new statutory requirements: provision of significant outreach services, preparation of a community health care and outreach needs assessment and plan, an independent board of directors, no discrimination with respect to government health plan participants, no discrimination in providing emergency services based on a patient's ability to pay, and provision of other free medically necessary care to the extent of the entity's financial ability.

This tax would have been equal to the greater of $25,000 or 5 percent of the organization's net investment income (including the net investment income of certain related supporting organizations) for the year.

TRADE LEGISLATION PROPOSAL

In the late summer of 1994, Congress for a time seemed to be on its way to using expected revenue from the implementation of intermediate sanctions as a means to help fund legislation to implement the Uruguay Round multilateral trade agreement (P.L. 103-465, 103d Cong., 2d Sess. (1994)). Although many expected intermediate sanctions as part of the health care reform bill, few expected it to be a part of the funding package for the General Agreement of Tariffs and Trade (GATT), where Congress was searching for $138 million. This proposal was tendered by the House conferees on the legislation to the Senate conferees on August 22, 1994 (BNA, *Daily Tax Report,* Aug. 23, 1994, at L-1, L-22). It was ultimately rejected on September 13, 1994 (BNA, *Daily Tax Report,* Sept. 14, 1994, at L-3, L-4), although the Uruguay Round Agreements Act was signed into law (P.L. 103-465, 103d Cong., 2d Sess. (1994)).

The proposal would have imposed penalty excise taxes as an intermediate sanction in cases where an organization, tax-exempt as a public charity or a social welfare organization, engaged in an *excess benefit transaction.* In these cases, intermediate sanctions could have been imposed on insiders (certain disqualified persons) who improperly benefited from an excess benefit transaction, and on organization managers who participated in the transaction knowing that it was improper.

An *excess benefit transaction* would have been defined as (1) any transaction in which an economic benefit is provided to, or for the use of, any disqualified person, if the value of the economic benefit provided to the person exceeds the value of consideration (including the performance of services) received by the organization for providing the benefit; (2) the lending of money or other extension of credit by an organization to, or for the use of, an organization manager; and (3) any transaction in which the amount of any economic benefit provided to, or for the use of, any disqualified person is determined in whole or in part by the gross or net income of one or more activities of the organization, provided that the transaction constitutes private inurement under existing law. Thus, excess benefit transactions subject to these taxes would have included transactions in which a disqualified person engages in a nonfair-market-value transaction with the organization or receives unreasonable compensation.

Existing tax law standards would have applied in determining reasonableness of compensation and fair market value. Legislative history would have indicated that the parties to the transaction would be entitled to rely on a rebuttable presumption of reasonableness with respect to a compensation arrangement with a disqualified person if the arrangement was approved by an independent board (or an independent committee authorized by the board) that: was composed entirely of individuals unrelated to and not subject to the control of the disqualified person(s) involved in the arrangement, obtained and relied on appropriate data as to comparability, and adequately documented the basis for its determination. As to the element of comparability, the factors would have included compensation levels paid by similarly situated organizations (both taxable and tax-exempt) for functionally comparable positions, the location of the organization (including the availability of similar specialties in the geographic area), independent compensation surveys by nationally recognized independent firms, or written offers from similar institutions competing for the services of the disqualified person.

A disqualified person who benefited from an excess benefit transaction would have been subject to a first-tier penalty tax equal to 25 percent of the amount of the excess benefit. Organization managers who participated in an excess benefit transaction, knowing that it was an improper transaction, would have been subject to a first-tier penalty tax of 10 percent of the amount of the excess benefit (subject to a maximum amount of tax of $10,000). Additional, second-tier taxes could have been imposed on a disqualified person if there was no correction of the excess benefit transaction within a specified time period. This penalty tax would have been 200 percent of the excess benefit.

The intermediate sanctions for excess benefit transactions could have been imposed by the IRS instead of or in addition to revocation of an organization's tax-exempt status. If more than one disqualified person or manager was liable for a penalty excise tax, all such persons would have been jointly and severally liable. The IRS would have had the authority to abate the excise tax penalty if it became established that the violation was due to reasonable cause and not to willful neglect and that the transaction was corrected within the correction period.

Further, the proposal would have imposed a tax on tax-exempt organizations that terminated their exempt status. The amount of this tax would have been equal to the lesser of the aggregate tax benefits that an organization can substantiate that it had received from its tax exemption or the value of the net assets of the organization. This tax would also have had an abatement feature.

Tax-exempt organizations would have been required to disclose on their annual information return information as the IRS may require with respect to excess benefit transactions, as well as any other excise tax penalties paid during the year (such as those for political expenditures or excess lobbying expenditures).

By this point, additional members of Congress, in the House of Representatives and the Senate, were taking an interest in intermediate sanctions (S. 2351, 103d Cong., 2d Sess. (1994); S. 2357, 103d Cong., 2d Sess. (1994); H.R. 613, 104th Cong., 1st Sess. (1995); H.R. 2316, 104th Cong., 1st Sess. (1995); H.R. 2517, 104th Cong., 1st Sess. (1995)).

SUBSEQUENT TREASURY PROPOSAL

Late in the summer of 1995, the Department of the Treasury sent to Capitol Hill still another version of an intermediate sanctions package, in an effort to revive attention to the concept. The proposal, unveiled on August 8, was accompanied by a letter to House Committee on Ways and Means Chairman Bill Archer (R-Tex.) from Assistant Secretary of the Treasury Samuels.

Under this scheme, a first-tier tax would have been imposed following any transaction in which a public charity or social welfare organization provided an *excess benefit* to a person who was in a position to exercise substantial influence over the affairs of the organization (a *controlling person*). The tax would have been imposed on the controlling person, not on the organization. An *excess benefit transaction* would have been one that provided, to or for the benefit of the controlling person, property or services the value of which exceeded that of the property or services the exempt organization received in turn. The excess benefit would thus have been the amount by which the controlling person's benefit exceeded the benefit received by the organization. For example, the payment by a public charity of excessive compensation to a controlling person would have been an excess benefit transaction

A second-tier tax would also have been imposed on the controlling person if that person failed to correct the excess benefit transaction before a notice of deficiency for the first-tier tax was mailed or the first-tier tax was assessed. Another tax would have been imposed on any organization manager who approved the excess benefit transaction, knowing it to be such a transaction. If the organization manager was also the controlling person in the excess benefit transaction, this separate tax would also have applied.

If an organization engaged in an excess benefit transaction and its tax exemption was subsequently revoked, these taxes would have continued to apply unless the organization paid a tax equal to the aggregate tax benefit it received while tax-exempt, or distributed its net assets to another exempt charitable or social welfare organization.

The payment of any of these taxes by the exempt organization on behalf of one of its controlling persons or managers would have constituted an excess benefit transaction unless the payment was treated as compensation to that person. The provision of insurance coverage, in the event of assessment of these taxes, by the exempt organization to its controlling persons or managers would not have been treated as an excess benefit transaction. The controlling persons or managers would have been permitted to exclude the insurance premiums from income, but they would have been required to include in income that portion of any payment under the insurance policy that covered an intermediate sanctions tax. In addition, rules similar to those governing permissible indemnification in the private foundation self-dealing context would have been developed.

The payment of compensation to a controlling person would not have constituted an excess benefit transaction if the amount of compensation was reasonable. Whether compensation for services or a payment for goods was reasonable would have depended on all of the relevant facts and circumstances. The standard for reasonable compensation would have been the same as that used to determine whether compensation was deductible as a business expense. The amount had to be that which a willing buyer would voluntarily pay a willing seller for the same or a comparable good or service. Benefits provided to a controlling person could have been justified as reasonable compensation only if the organization in fact provided the benefits as compensation for services at the time they were paid. The determination as to whether a benefit was intended to be compensatory was to be based on all of the facts and circumstances.

A transaction that did not directly transfer goods or services to a controlling person would, nevertheless, have been for the benefit of that controlling person if the recipient of the goods or services would be a disqualified person under the existing private foundation rules. This would have entailed those who are certain family members of the controlling person or an entity in which the controlling person had at least a 35 percent interest.

An intermediate sanction would not have been provided for transactions that yielded excess benefits to noncontrolling parties. This area, then, would have been left—particularly with respect to public charities—to the vicissitudes of applicability of the private benefit doctrine.

The controlling person receiving the excess benefit, or for whose benefit it was supplied, would have been subject to the two-tier tax. If more than one controlling person was involved, there would have been joint and several liability for the tax. Organization managers who knowingly participated in excess benefit transactions would have been subject to the separate tax on organization managers. The organization would not have been subject to a tax. However, if the organization's tax exemption was revoked, it would have had the option of paying a tax in lieu of continuing to have its controlling persons subject to the intermediate sanctions excise taxes.

The first tier of the tax imposed on a controlling person would have equaled 25 percent of the excess benefit. The second tier of the tax on a controlling person would have equaled 200 percent of the excess benefit, plus interest. The tax on the organization manager would have equaled 10 percent of the excess benefit, up to a maximum of $10,000.

The second-tier tax on the controlling person would have been waived or refunded if the controlling person returned the excess benefit to the exempt organization before the first-tier tax was assessed or a notice of deficiency was mailed. The first-tier tax could have been waived or refunded if there was reasonable cause for the excess benefit transaction.

A rebuttable presumption would have arisen to the effect that a transaction was not an excess benefit one if the exempt organization's board had (1) delegated authority to make decisions with respect to the transaction to those board members who did not have a conflict of interest; (2) considered specific information relevant to the decision, including as much information on comparable transactions as could be collected through reasonable efforts; (3) documented the basis for its decision; and (4) approved the transaction, including a limit on the total amount that could be transferred to the controlling person in advance of its occurrence.

The intermediate sanctions taxes would have been applicable in addition to, rather than exclusively as a substitute for, revocation of tax-exempt status. However, the intermediate sanctions excise tax would have been the sole sanction available in those cases in which the excess benefit did not rise to a level where it called into question whether the organization was a qualified tax-exempt entity. Revocation, with or without the excise tax, would have been an appropriate sanction only when the organization no longer operated primarily as an exempt organization.

1995 TAX AND BUDGET BILL

On September 19, 1995, the House Committee on Ways and Means adopted a tax and spending bill that included an intermediate sanctions proposal (H.R. 2491, 104th Cong., 1st Sess. (1995)). This intermediate sanctions package was essentially the same as that previously proposed by the Department of the Treasury. The following changes or additions were made to the Treasury package: (1) the term *disqualified person* was to be used rather than *controlling person;* (2) disqualified persons would include siblings and their spouses (unlike the private foundation rules) and any individual who was in a position to exercise substantial influence over the affairs of the organization; (3) the Department of the Treasury was to promptly issue guidance on and examples of "revenue-sharing arrangements" that are excess benefit transactions; (4) transactions involving subsidiaries would be taken into account; (5) the IRS would have the authority to abate the excise tax penalties where the violation is due to reasonable cause and not due to willful neglect and the transaction at issue is corrected within the specified period, and (6) the sanctions generally would apply to excess benefit transactions occurring on or after September 14, 1995.

As to this latter item, however, the sanctions would not have applied to any transaction pursuant to a written contract for the performance of personal services which was binding on September 13, 1995, and at all times thereafter before the transaction occurred, and the terms of which have not materially changed.

The Senate version of this legislation did not contain the intermediate sanctions provisions. The sanctions were in the final version of the legislation (see H. Rep. No. 350, 104th Cong., 1st Sess. (II) (1995)), which passed Congress and was vetoed.

For a time, it appeared that intermediate sanctions would have to await resolution of the political stalemate over tax and budget legislation. Another possibility was that they would be part of some other significant tax bill. (Still another intermediate sanctions bill was introduced, however (H.R. 3903, 104th Cong., 2d Sess. (1996)).)

In early 1996, the Clinton Administration issued its budget proposal for fiscal year 1997 which contained intermediate sanctions legislation.

In the meantime, a bipartisan item of legislation was making its way through Congress and on to enactment: the "Taxpayer Bill of Rights 2." This measure provided for increased protection of taxpayer rights in complying with the federal tax laws and in dealing with the IRS in its administration of these laws. It established, among many other features, a Taxpayer Advocate within the IRS; revised the rules pertaining to abatement of interest and penalties; increased the limit on recovery of civil damages for unauthorized collection actions; and provided relief from retroactive application of federal tax regulations.

This legislative package, to be revenue-neutral, required funds to pay for these and other provisions. One of these "revenue offsets" was the set of rules for intermediate sanctions. These rules are estimated by the Department of the Treasury to generate $33 million over the course of fiscal years 1996–2002.

The Taxpayer Bill of Rights 2 (H.R. 2337, 104th Cong., 2d Sess. (1996)) was favorably reported out of the House Committee on Ways and Means on March 28, 1996 (H. Rep. 104-506, 104th Cong., 2d Sess. (1996)). This legislation—symbolically considered by the House of Representatives during the week of April 15—passed the House on April 16, 1996. The identical legislation passed the Senate by means of the unanimous consent procedure on July 11, 1996. There was no report from the Senate Committee on Finance and, because of the unanimity of the Senate, no report from a conference committee. With little fanfare, the proposed legislation—one of the most significant bodies of law ever created to directly impact public charities—was signed into law on July 30, 1996.

Form 4720 (1995)

Form **4720**	**Return of Certain Excise Taxes on Charities and Other Persons Under Chapters 41 and 42 of the Internal Revenue Code** (Sections 4911, 4912, 4941, 4942, 4943, 4944, 4945, and 4955) ▶ See separate instructions.	OMB No. 1545-0052 **1995**
Department of the Treasury Internal Revenue Service		

For calendar year 1995 or other tax year beginning _____, 1995, and ending _____, 19____

Name of foundation or public charity	Employer identification number

Number, street, and room or suite no. (or P.O. box if mail is not delivered to street address)	Check box for type of annual return: ☐ Form 990 ☐ Form 990-EZ
City or town, state, and ZIP code	☐ Form 990-PF
	☐ Form 5227

		Yes	No
A	Is the organization a foreign private foundation within the meaning of section 4948(b)?....................		
B	Has corrective action been taken on any transaction that resulted in Chapter 42 taxes being reported on this form?		

If "Yes," attach a detailed documentation and description of the corrective action taken and, if applicable, enter the fair market value of any property recovered as a result of the correction ▶ $_____ . For any uncorrected acts, attach explanation (see page 3 of the instructions).

Part I   Taxes on Private Foundation or Public Charity (Sections 4911(a), 4912(a), 4942(a), 4943(a), 4944(a)(1), 4945(a)(1), and 4955(a)(1))

1	Tax on undistributed income—Schedule B, line 4	1	
2	Tax on excess business holdings—Schedule C, line 7	2	
3	Tax on investments that jeopardize charitable purpose—Schedule D, Part I, column (e) ...	3	
4	Tax on taxable expenditures—Schedule E, Part I, column (g)	4	
5	Tax on political expenditures—Schedule F, Part I, column (e)	5	
6	Tax on excess lobbying expenditures—Schedule G, line 4	6	
7	Tax on disqualifying lobbying expenditures—Schedule H, Part I, column (e)	7	
8	Total (add lines 1-7)	8	

Part II-A   Taxes on Self-Dealers, Foundation Managers, and Organization Managers (Sections 4912(b), 4941(a), 4944(a)(2), 4945(a)(2), and 4955(a)(2))

	(a) Name and address of person subject to tax	(b) Taxpayer identifying number
a		
b		
c		
d		

	(c) Tax on self-dealing— Schedule A, Part II, col. (d), and Part III, col. (d)	(d) Tax on investments that jeopardize charitable purpose—Schedule D, Part II, col. (d)	(e) Tax on taxable expenditures— Schedule E, Part II, col. (d)	(f) Tax on political expenditures— Schedule F, Part II, col. (d)
a				
b				
c				
d				
Total				

	(g) Tax on disqualifying lobbying expenditures—Schedule H, Part II, col. (d)	(h) Total—Add cols. (c) through (g)
a		
b		
c		
d		
Total		

Part II-B   Summary of Taxes (See Tax Payments on page 2 of the instructions)

1	Enter the total taxes listed in Part II-A, column (h), that apply to self-dealers, foundation managers, and organization managers who sign this form. If all sign, enter the total amount from Part II-A, column (h)	1	
2	Total tax. Add Part I, line 8, and Part II-B, line 1. (Make check(s) or money order(s) payable to the Internal Revenue Service.)	2	

For Paperwork Reduction Act Notice, see page 1 of the instructions.   Form **4720** (1995)
ISA

STF FED5191F.1

Form 4720 (1995)

155

SCHEDULE A—Initial Taxes on Self-Dealing (Section 4941)

Part I — Acts of Self-Dealing and Tax Computation

(a) Act number	(b) Date of act	(c) Description of act
1		
2		
3		
4		
5		

(d) Question number from Form 990-PF, Part VII-B, or Form 5227, Part VI-B, applicable to the act	(e) Amount involved in act	(f) Initial tax on self-dealing (5% of col. (e))	(g) Tax on foundation managers (if applicable) (lesser of $10,000 or 2½% of col. (e))

Part II — Summary of Tax Liability of Self-Dealers and Proration of Payments

(a) Names of self-dealers liable for tax	(b) Act no. from Part I, col. (a)	(c) Tax from Part I, col. (f), or prorated amount	(d) Self-dealer's total tax liability (add amounts in col. (c)) (see page 4 of the instructions)

Part III — Summary of Tax Liability of Foundation Managers and Proration of Payments

(a) Names of foundation managers liable for tax	(b) Act no. from Part I, col. (a)	(c) Tax from Part I, col. (g), or prorated amount	(d) Manager's total tax liability (add amounts in col. (c)) (see page 4 of the instructions)

SCHEDULE B—Initial Tax on Undistributed Income (Section 4942)

1	Undistributed income for years before 1994 (from Form 990-PF for 1995, Part XIII, line 6d) .	1	
2	Undistributed income for 1994 (from Form 990-PF for 1995, Part XIII, line 6e)	2	
3	Total undistributed income at end of current tax year beginning in 1995 and subject to tax under section 4942 (add lines 1 and 2)	3	
4	Tax—Enter 15% of line 3 here and on page 1, Part I, line 1	4	

SCHEDULE C—Initial Tax on Excess Business Holdings (Section 4943)

Business Holdings and Computation of Tax

If you have taxable excess holdings in more than one business enterprise, attach a separate schedule for each enterprise. Refer to the instructions on page 6 for each line item before making any entries.

Name and address of business enterprise

Employer identification number . . . . ▶

Form of enterprise (corporation, partnership, trust, joint venture, sole proprietorship, etc.) . . . . . ▶

		(a) Voting stock (profits interest or beneficial interest)	(b) Value	(c) Nonvoting stock (capital interest)
1	Foundation holdings in business enterprise **1**	%	%	
2	Permitted holdings in business enterprise **2**	%	%	
3	Value of excess holdings in business enterprise . **3**			
4	Value of excess holdings disposed of within 90 days; or, other value of excess holdings not subject to section 4943 tax (attach explanation) . **4**			
5	Taxable excess holdings in business enterprise—line 3 minus line 4 . . . . **5**			
6	Tax—Enter 5% of line 5 . . . . **6**			
7	**Total tax** — Add amounts on line 6, columns (a), (b), and (c); enter total here and on page 1, Part I, line 2 . . . . **7**			

SCHEDULE D—Initial Taxes on Investments That Jeopardize Charitable Purpose (Section 4944)

Part I   **Investments and Tax Computation**

(a) Investment number	(b) Date of investment	(c) Description of investment	(d) Amount of investment	(e) Initial tax on foundation (5% of col. (d))	(f) Initial tax on foundation managers (if applicable)— (lesser of $5,000 or 5% of col. (d))
1					
2					
3					
4					
5					

Total—column (e). Enter here and on page 1, Part I, line 3 . . . .

Total—column (f). Enter total (or prorated amount) here and in Part II, column (c), below . . . .

Part II   **Summary of Tax Liability of Foundation Managers and Proration of Payments**

(a) Names of foundation managers liable for tax	(b) Investment no. from Part I, col. (a)	(c) Tax from Part I, col. (f), or prorated amount	(d) Manager's total tax liability (add amounts in col. (c)) (see page 7 of the instructions)

STF FED5191F.3

SCHEDULE E—Initial Taxes on Taxable Expenditures (Section 4945)

Part I Expenditures and Computation of Tax

(a) Item number	(b) Amount	(c) Date paid or incurred	(d) Name and address of recipient	(e) Description of expenditure and purposes for which made
1				
2				
3				
4				
5				

(f) Question number from Form 990-PF, Part VII-B, or Form 5227, Part VI-B, applicable to the expenditure	(g) Initial tax imposed on foundation (10% of col. (b))	(h) Initial tax imposed on foundation managers (if applicable)—(lesser of $5,000 or 2½% of col. (b))
Total—column (g). Enter here and on page 1, Part I, line 4		
Total—column (h). Enter total (or prorated amount) here and in Part II, column (c), below		

Part II Summary of Tax Liability of Foundation Managers and Proration of Payments

(a) Names of foundation managers liable for tax	(b) Item no. from Part I, col. (a)	(c) Tax from Part I, col. (h), or prorated amount	(d) Manager's total tax liability (add amounts in col. (c)) (see page 7 of the instructions)

SCHEDULE F—Initial Taxes on Political Expenditures (Section 4955)

Part I Expenditures and Computation of Tax

(a) Item number	(b) Amount	(c) Date paid or incurred	(d) Description of political expenditure	(e) Initial tax imposed on organization or foundation (10% of col. (b))	(f) Initial tax imposed on managers (if applicable) (lesser of $5,000 or 2½% of col. (b))
1					
2					
3					
4					
5					

Total—column (e). Enter here and on page 1, Part I, line 5 . . . .

Total—column (f). Enter total (or prorated amount) here and in Part II, column (c), below . . . .

Part II Summary of Tax Liability of Organization Managers or Foundation Managers and Proration of Payments

(a) Names of organization managers or foundation managers liable for tax	(b) Item no. from Part I, col. (a)	(c) Tax from Part I, col. (f), or prorated amount	(d) Manager's total tax liability (add amounts in col. (c)) (see page 8 of the instructions)

STF FED5191F.4

SCHEDULE G—Tax on Excess Lobbying Expenditures (Section 4911)

1	Excess of grassroots expenditures over grassroots nontaxable amount (from Schedule A (Form 990), Part VI-A, column (b), line 43). (See page 8 of the instructions before making entry.)	**1**
2	Excess of lobbying expenditures over lobbying nontaxable amount (from Schedule A (Form 990), Part VI-A, column (b), line 44). (See page 8 of the instructions before making entry.)	**2**
3	Taxable lobbying expenditures—enter the larger of line 1 or line 2	**3**
4	Tax—Enter 25% of line 3 here and on page 1, Part I, line 6	**4**

SCHEDULE H—Taxes on Disqualifying Lobbying Expenditures (Section 4912)

Part I **Expenditures and Computation of Tax**

(a) Item number	(b) Amount	(c) Date paid or incurred	(d) Description of lobbying expenditures	(e) Tax imposed on organization (5% of col. (b))	(f) Tax imposed on organization managers (if applicable)— (5% of col. (b))
1					
2					
3					
4					
5					

Total—column (e). Enter here and on page 1, Part I, line 7 ....

Total—column (f). Enter total (or prorated amount) here and in Part II, column (c), below ....

Part II **Summary of Tax Liability of Organization Managers and Proration of Payments**

(a) Names of organization managers liable for tax	(b) Item no. from Part I, col. (a)	(c) Tax from Part I, col. (f), or prorated amount	(d) Manager's total tax liability (add amounts in col. (c)) (see page 8 of the instructions)

Under penalties of perjury, I declare that I have examined this return, including accompanying schedules and statements, and to the best of my knowledge and belief it is true, correct, and complete. Declaration of preparer (other than taxpayer) is based on all information of which preparer has any knowledge.

Signature of officer or trustee	Title	Date

Signature (and organization name if applicable) of self-dealer, foundation manager, or organization manager	Date

Signature (and organization name if applicable) of self-dealer, foundation manager, or organization manager	Date

Signature (and organization name if applicable) of self-dealer, foundation manager, or organization manager	Date

Signature of individual or firm preparing the return	Address of preparer	Date

STF FED5191F.5

APPENDIX E

Determining the Reasonableness of Compensation: Structuring the Analysis

The following analysis was prepared by William C. Mercer, Inc., an international firm specializing in the design and implementation of compensation and benefit programs, and is reprinted with permission.

A. DEFINING THE SCOPE OF THE SANCTIONS

The first and arguably most complex set of issues that have to be answered are which individuals and which transactions should be covered under the scope of work, i.e., who are the *disqualified persons* and what, potentially, is an *excess benefit transaction*? We advise that the client's legal counsel participate in determining which individuals and specific transactions come under review. In doing so, we should recognize that each organization will have its own level of tolerance for the exposure presented by the legislation. Thus, some will be interested in taking a very broad view of the issue—including all individuals who might be deemed to be in a position to "exercise substantial influence" and all possible transactions. On the other hand, some may be only interested in containing the analysis to a select few individuals and very specific transactions. Unless directed otherwise, consultants should advise the broadest view possible, for this offers the greatest protection for the organizations.

In determining the scope of the analysis, these questions should be explored:

1. Which persons might be considered as a *disqualified person*?
2. Who is an *organization manager*?
3. To which organizational entities does the law apply?
4. Which transactions are most likely to come under scrutiny?

Official guidance has not yet been provided on intermediate sanctions and much uncertainty remains. Clients should understand that there are open issues. However, here are a few key concepts:

- *Disqualified Persons*

    A *disqualified person* is any individual who is, at any time during the 5-year period ending on the date of an excess benefit transaction, "in a position to exercise substantial influence over the affairs of the organization." In the context of a healthcare organization, for example, the broadest interpretation would include any individual in a position to direct, control, or substantially influence:

    1. The strategic direction of the organization;
    2. The use, acquisition and/or disposition of financial, physical, clinical, and human resources;
    3. Committing the organization to substantial liability; and
    4. Policy-making.

    Physicians, while considered *insiders* for purposes of *private inurement*, are not always considered *disqualified persons*. To be considered as such, they must also be in a position to exercise substantial influence over the affairs of the organization. However, the legislation is likely to apply to physicians acting in an executive capacity. Furthermore, transactions involving the acquisition of physician practices and/or revenue-sharing arrangements (e.g., incentive plans) may come under scrutiny.

    Guidance could be helpful from organizational design consultants who will be familiar with the nature and scope of executive roles and can assist in determining disqualified persons.

- *Organization Manager*

  An *organization manager* is defined according to a functional test but generally will include any director, trustee, or officer who participated in the decision to enter into an excess benefit transaction.

  Under the *rebuttable presumption,* it is important to establish the "independence" of the *organization manager.* It must be demonstrated that the director is unrelated to and not subject to the control of the *disqualified person.* It is clear that "cronyism" arising from interlocking board relationships (e.g., when the CEO of a hospital is a board member of another charity, and that charity's CEO is a board member of the hospital) will cause these individuals to not be considered *independent.* However, it is not clear how the *independence* question will be resolved in the case of a business relationship. For example, a lawyer or a consultant whose firm provides services to the organization may or may not be considered an independent director. Legal counsel should be involved in this issue.

- *Organizational Entities*

  It is clear that the excise taxes apply where an excess benefit is provided *directly or indirectly* by a tax-exempt organization. Technical employment and payroll relationships do not appear to matter—the IRS will apply substance over form. Thus, for example, an individual who technically is an employee of a taxable entity (e.g., a physician clinic) that is part of a larger organization including section 501(c)(3) or (c)(4) organizations may not escape tax merely because of that technical relationship. Here again, the involvement of counsel is important to sort out the organizational structure and underlying relationships and risks.

- *Potential Excess Benefit Transactions*

  All of the following comes within the scope of the intermediate sanctions rules and are likely to draw the most scrutiny:

  1. *Cash compensation*—in the form of salary, bonus/incentive payments under an annual or long-term incentive, sign-on bonus, car allowance, etc.

  2. *Benefits and perquisites of substantial monetary value not available to broader workforce or as matter of policy*—non-qualified supplemental retirement plans, other forms of deferred compensation, forgiveness of indebtedness to employer, personal entertainment and travel expenses not related to the conduct

of business, purchase of luxury items, personal loans at interest rates substantially below prevailing levels, "gross-ups," etc.

3. *Transactions at other than fair market value*—transfer of an asset for an amount in excess of or at less than fair market value—for example, the acquisition of a physician practice with substantial "goodwill" factored into the purchase price and not substantiated through independent appraisal.

4. *Revenue-sharing arrangement*—under regulations to be issued by the IRS, any arrangement that appears to be nothing more than an attempt to divert profits to insiders and/or arrangements where the compensation is based either on gross or net income.

It appears that all amounts denominated by a Board of compensation committee as "compensation" and reported as such on applicable forms (e.g., Forms W-2, 1099 and 1040) will be treated as such, and that reasonableness will be analyzed by the IRS on a total compensation basis. Only the unreasonable portion will be subject to taxes. In contrast, transactions outside the scope of compensation—e.g., an executive's free or below-market use of an organization-owned apartment—can result in tax on 100 percent of the value of the benefit.

B. ELEMENTS OF THE ANALYSIS: INTERMEDIATE SANCTIONS AND ALIGNMENT ISSUES AS NATURAL COMPLEMENTS

In order to responsibly answer the critical questions relating to intermediate sanctions and alignment issues, we suggest a comprehensive analytical approach. The following model outlines the construct and process consultants should employ. This process is intended to serve as a best practices guideline for approaching the issue. The final form of the analysis and the process should be determined based on client needs and interests.

Overall Organizational/Business Strategy Analysis

Ultimately, we may be asked to comment on whether the client's approach is both reasonable from a compliance perspective and rational as a business proposition. Obviously, the question of executive compensation alignment can only be answered in light of the client's business strategy.

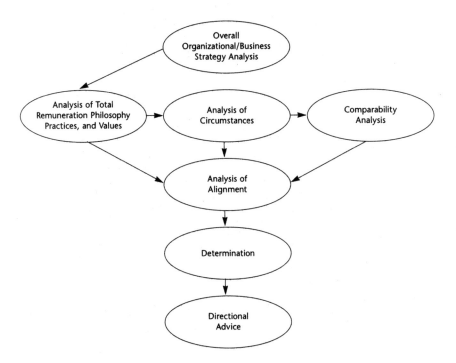

In order to understand a client's organizational strategy, it is necessary to first understand the dynamics of the market(s) that creates the impetus for the direction it has chosen. For example, in healthcare organizations, there currently is a battle for market share waged on local fronts, each evolving at its own pace. Therefore, the stage and pace of evolution and ultimate configuration of the market dictates to a large degree the direction of health plans and providers. Using healthcare as an example, the table on the following page should be helpful to a consultant's understanding of market dynamics influencing organizational direction.

Stage of Local Market Evolution in Healthcare

In analyzing the market dynamics, the consultant should ask the following questions:

1. What stage of evolution is the client's market currently in?
2. In what stage will the market ultimately end up?
3. How long will it take to occur (i.e., what is the strategic time-frame)?

	Stage I: Unstructured	Stage II: Loose Framework	Stage III: Consolidation	Stage IV: Managed Competition
Characteristics	• Dominated by major indemnity insurers • Few provider "systems" • Over capacity of beds, specialists, medical technology	• Proliferation of HMOs/PPOs • Beginning formation of provider "networks" • Bed capacity declining uniformly across competitors	• Shake out of marginal players • Emergence of a few dominant HMOs • Formalized "systems" developing • Provider/payor alliances forming	• Fewer HMOs in each regional market • Fully integrated systems • Solidified provider/payor alliances • Direct employer/provider contracts
HMO Penetration	Less than 10%	10–30%	30–50%	50%
Pricing	Fee for service	Fee for service, discount, per diem	Per diem, per case, physician capitation	Cost per covered life per health system
Basis for Purchasing	Encounter, cost of claim	Encounter, cost of claim	Cost per covered life per health plan	Beneficiary health status, total health care cost
Basis of Competition	Service, technology	Service, price	Price	Price, outcomes
Market Examples (Currently in Stage)	• Rural communities • Small communities isolated from large urban centers	• Mid-size Southern cities • "Bedroom" communities	• Atlanta • Dallas • Chicago	• California • Hawaii • Boston • Minneapolis

The answer to these questions will put the client's direction in perspective and help explain the specific change initiatives they are pursuing. It will also lend considerable insight into the leadership dimension of the organization and its compensation philosophy and practices. For example:

Large hospital in a mid-size urban market where managed care penetration is increasing at a very rapid pace commits to a strategic direction of becoming an integrated delivery system. CEO and Board conclude that several members of executive staff are critical to the direction and must be retained and new executives from more developed markets have to be acquired in the immediate future. The Board advises the CEO to "pay what you have to" to secure the necessary talent.

A nationally known charity is nearly bankrupt having become seen as ineffective and powerless. The Board decides the mission is still valid and new energy, leadership and image building is needed. The Board initiates a search for a national figure, highly respected and affiliated with the charity's mission. They must be a leader, manager and spiritual rescuer. The Board will pay (total compensation) what it has to knowing the alternative is to cease existing.

The operating hypotheses should be that each organization will respond to market pressure in their own, perhaps unique way. This includes how they structure executive remuneration. For example, we should not assume that stage I and IV healthcare organizations will or should structure compensation in the same way. Similarly, a charity emerging from crisis and in need of highly skilled, stable management should build a competitive reward strategy around these objectives. The source for this talent (competitive market), the need to retain this talent over time, the affordability of various reward options and other considerations would drive the development of a "reasonable" package. This package might *not* be "reasonable" or appropriate for a similar organization not seeking crisis management/turnaround talent.

Understanding business strategy will also provide a foundation for evaluating the specifics of the compensation strategy including the mix of total remuneration, which is critical to both the determination of reasonableness, and our ability to provide directional advice on the alignment issue.

Analysis of Total Remuneration Philosophy, Practices, and Values

Since the legislation defines "compensation" broadly to include health and welfare, retirement benefits, and perquisites, it is necessary to approach the work from a total remuneration perspective. To advise for the future, it is important to consider the board's philosophy, how it has governed the process, and what sources of data have been used to establish comparability. The analysis should focus on:

1. Understanding the Board's philosophy about total remuneration including:

   - How the competitive market has been defined;
   - The targeted level of competitiveness of each of the elements of total remuneration;
   - The board's view of variable/incentive pay; and
   - The mix of remuneration.

2. Understanding how total remuneration has been governed, including:

   - Is there a Compensation Committee?
   - Are the voting members of the Compensation Committee independent?
   - Is there a clear delineation of responsibilities between the Compensation Committee and the CEO?
   - Are there external advisors that have presented independent recommendations and data sources?
   - Have decisions been documented?

3. Determining the value of each element of the client's total remuneration package, including:

   - Cash compensation;
   - Incentive plan structure;
   - Health and welfare benefits;
   - Retirement benefits;
   - Nonqualified supplemental retirement benefits;

- Perquisites; and
- Loans and similar transactions.

Although the reasonableness of compensation is evaluated on the basis of total compensation, it is also important to ensure that no element of compensation is unreasonable, in and of itself. "Cash compensation" should include the annualized base salary value plus any payments or accruals under an annual or long-term incentive plan, plus any other form of taxable income (e.g., car allowances). Non-statutory health and welfare benefits do not necessarily require a valuation. The analysis should focus on identifying "red flags" through a review of the prevalence of the plan type, and design characteristics. The analysis of qualified and nonqualified retirement plans should focus on determining the employer's actual outlay, income-replacement ratios, the prevalence of the vehicle used, and the reasonableness of the employer's liability. It is true, however, that we should consider any executive-only benefit and in particular a nonqualified/supplemental pension plan always to be a "red flag" requiring further analysis. However, valuation may be required of both executive-only benefits, as well as the employee-wide benefits provided to the disqualified persons if either the executive-only benefits appear out of line or the entire compensation package appears out of line. For performance and rewards consultants, additional guidance will be needed here from health and welfare and retirement consultants as to appropriate valuation methodology.

Analysis of Circumstances

In evaluating whether the client can establish the "rebuttable presumption" it is important to understand the issues and circumstances that led the organization to do what it did. We've discussed the need to understand the impact of market dynamics on organizational strategy and the potential implications for executive remuneration. Other organizational dimensions can also impact the board's thinking and decisions. For example:

- How has the organization performed?
- Has sufficient progress been made towards achieving strategic results?
- Does the organization have the necessary leadership talent?
- Are the economic incentives properly aligned? (With each other? With the organization's mission and operational strategy?)

Issues specific to particular individuals should be explored. Some examples:

- Was an incumbent recruited into a position of strategic importance to the organization, which required the organization to offer highly competitive compensation and/or extend certain guarantees?
- Was an incumbent's compensation adjusted to assure equity with other members of the executive staff?
- Was the organization at risk of losing an incumbent at a time that would have had significant negative impact on the organization?
- Was an incumbent asked to assume a position that would greatly encumber his/her personal life?
- Did an incumbent contribute substantially to the achievement of a critical business result?

Analysis of Comparability

Although we believe the intermediate sanctions rules and alignment issues are natural complements, it is important to remember that the focus of the rebuttable presumption of reasonableness is comparability. Therefore, assessment of the elements of remuneration at the client organization, in light of market practices and competitive levels, is a very critical step. The most important determinations are establishing the proper comparison group and identifying the available sources of data for credible comparison. Examples of advisable criteria for determining comparability are:

1. That the organizations operate within the same market evolution stage;
2. That they have similar operating characteristics; and
3. That they operate within the same recruiting markets.

In some cases, the compensation committee of the Board may have already determined the group and the data sources (particularly for cash compensation). In these instances, the consultant should evaluate the determination in light of his or her understanding of organizational strategy, organizational philosophy, and the general circumstances. The consultant should focus on answering three basic questions:

- Is the determination of the comparative group and data sources reasonable?

- What has and has not been considered?
- What were the alternatives?

For example, assume an organization has adopted a compensation strategy intended to deliver highly competitive compensation predicated on comparable levels of organizational performance. However, neither the comparative groups or the data sources used actually take performance into account. The consultant should work with the client to establish a better group and data source whose performance is comparable. (This, of course, assumes that the relationship between organizational performance and executive compensation is at least somewhat linear.)

In the event that the organization cannot specifically point to the data source(s) on which they have relied to base executive compensation decisions, the consultant will need to raise this as a key issue and attempt to make this determination. In doing so, the consultant will have to reconcile what he or she understands about the organization with the availability of credible data. As a general rule of thumb, the more sources of data that can be consulted the more likely that the truest "picture" of market practice will emerge.

It is important for Mercer to take a very activist approach to comparability. We need to make sure that we are conducting a series of individual analyses and reaching a determination for each case. We need to establish the best possible comparison based on what we understand and the available sources of data. Depending on the position and the elements of remuneration that are under review, we may end up relying on multiple sources of data. This is not inherently problematic to the extent that we can put forth a reasonable argument as to why the analysis was structured as such and why the data source(s) were chosen. The key is to understand the strength of the comparison, the credibility of the data and the degree to which it supports the remuneration actually provided.

As suggested earlier, it is essential that we understand the nature of each "disqualified person's" role in the organization. Doing so will assure that we are in a position to judge the degree to which particular comparability data is appropriate for the position in question. The "job analysis" should focus on:

1. The breadth of the person's impact:
   - System-wide v. entity-specific
   - Single v. multiple functions
   - Homogenous v. diverse functions

2. The nature and parameters of decision-making:
   - Approve v. recommend
3. The magnitude of resources controlled/impacted
4. The relative complexity of business issues

Analysis of Alignment

The fundamental questions that should be answered as part of this analysis are:

- Is compensation structured in a manner that reinforces the strategic direction and key organizational results?
- Does it encourage behaviors consistent with the values at the organization?

Here are some things to look for that might suggest that it is not.

1. Lack of processes or mechanisms that translate strategic objectives to performance expectations like a performance-based incentive compensation plan, or a robust executive performance management process.
2. Misaligned performance measures at the organizational or individual level that encourage sub-optimization.
3. Lack of alignment between performance measures for the short and long term incentive plans.
4. Over-emphasis on financial and operating measures to the point that the importance of other key measures is diminished.
5. Compensation opportunities that do not provide sufficient motivation.
6. Compensation opportunities that do not increase as organizational performance increases.
7. Compensation structured in such a fashion that it may encourage behavior that is not consistent with the values of the organization.
8. Compensation practices that promote the perception of inequity.
9. Compensation practices that are not sufficiently competitive.

C. DETERMINATION (WRITTEN OPINIONS)

For intermediate sanctions purposes, Mercer, or Mercer in conjunction with counsel, will be asked to render an opinion as to the reasonableness of practices involving individuals. In rendering the opinion, we should be sure to document the following:

1. Restatement of the purpose and scope of analysis (consistent with the initial Letter of Understanding and any subsequent developments);
2. Specific learnings about the organization and circumstances;
3. Sources of information;
4. Any working assumptions;
5. The analytical methodology;
6. Findings that support our conclusions; and
7. Reasons why possible alternatives were rejected.

When documenting findings and conclusions, keep in mind that this should be done for each individual ("disqualified person" or "organization manager"). It is not necessary (unless directed by the client) to offer a conclusion on the overall reasonableness of the entire approach.

Here are some suggestions/thoughts to keep in mind when preparing the opinion:

1. There may be advantages to the client to structure the engagement through its lawyer. The question of the importance of lawyer-client privilege issues to the project, and how best to obtain the privilege, should be raised with the client and its legal counsel.
2. Prior to submitting a formal and final opinion, the consultant should review the findings with the client and the client's lawyer.
3. At some point, we may be asked to provide expert testimony on the client's behalf. We can expect to have to defend that which we document. Therefore, care should be exercised to assure that the writing is clear, crisp, concise and all statements of fact be defensible.
4. Mercer cannot assure "compliance" with the intermediate sanctions rules and its rebuttable presumption of reasonableness. Words must be chosen carefully so as to avoid any implication that we are providing such an assurance.
5. The final opinion and/or report should be peer reviewed.

Following is an example of a template capturing the elements of a Total Remuneration Philosophy and Strategy. While oversimplified, it nonetheless will give one a sense of the general substance.

Total Remuneration Philosophy

1. Total remuneration levels and design will be consistent with the organization's tax-exempt purpose.

2. Cash compensation opportunities will be directly linked to organizational performance. Base salaries will be market-competitive with additional opportunities based on organizational performance.

3. Incentives (short-term and long-term) will be the principle vehicle by which we align organizational performance and rewards.

4. Executives must demonstrate behaviors consistent with the values of the organization to earn salary increases.

5. Opportunities to earn incentive compensation will be based primarily on a "common fate" philosophy. We will recognize individual performance and contribution, but not to the same extent that we will recognize the performance of the organization.

6. Health, welfare, and retirement benefits will be market-competitive and assure adequate levels of income protection and replacement. Cost-sharing arrangements will be consistent with industry norms.

7. Executive perquisites will be provided only to the extent they are customary and consistent with the values of the organization.

8. Employment contracts will be extended to key contributors and reflect customary terms and provisions.

The next steps in the process would be to develop a "blueprint" to each of the "programs" needed to support the direction. Beyond the "blueprint" the client may require consulting assistance in the actual design and implementation.

Glossary

Terms in italics appear elsewhere in the Glossary.

Abate. The IRS has the authority to abate the *intermediate sanctions initial excise tax* in certain circumstances, principally where a taxable event was due to *reasonable cause* and not to willful neglect (IRC § 4962(a)). In general, the word "abatement" means an alleviation, lessening, mitigation, or reduction of something.

Additional excise tax. The *intermediate sanctions* "additional excise tax" is a tax of 200 percent of the amount of an *excess benefit* received by a *disqualified person* from an *applicable tax-exempt organization*. The tax is imposed where an *initial excise tax* was assessed and there was no *correction* of the excess benefit within the *taxable period* (IRC § 4958(b)). This tax is also known as a "second-tier tax."

Annual information return. Nearly every *tax-exempt organization* is required to file an "annual information return" with the IRS (IRC § 6033(b)). The return filed by most organizations is *Form 990;* smaller organizations may file *Form 990-EZ*.

Applicable tax-exempt organization. An "applicable tax-exempt organization" is a *public charity* or a *social welfare organization,* including an organization described in either of these categories of exempt organizations at any time during the five-year period ending on the date of the transaction (IRC § 4958(e)(2)).

Hopkins, *The Law of Tax-Exempt Organizations* (6th ed.; New York: John Wiley & Sons, Inc., 1992) is referenced throughout as *Tax-Exempt Organizations.* Other words and phrases not in this Glossary may be found in Hopkins, *The Nonprofit Law Dictionary* (John Wiley & Sons, Inc., 1994).

Articles of organization. The term "articles of organization" is used to describe the document by which a *tax-exempt organization* is created. Usually, this document is articles of incorporation, a declaration of trust, or a constitution.

Business league. A "business league" is an organization that is *tax-exempt* because it is described in IRC § 501(c)(6). A business league is an association of persons having some common business interest, the purpose of which is to promote that common interest; its activities are directed toward the improvement of business conditions of one or more lines of business. This category of tax exemption is the subject of Chapter 29 of *Tax-Exempt Organizations.*

Captive board. A "captive board" is a board of trustees or board of directors of a *tax-exempt organization* that is comprised of one or more individuals who are related (by a family or business relationship) to the individual who received from the organization an economic benefit that is under scrutiny.

Closing agreement. A "closing agreement" is an agreement that the IRS enters into with a person, relating to the liability of that person with respect to a tax for a particular period (IRC § 7121).

Combined voting power. The term "combined voting power" includes voting power represented by holdings of voting stock, actual or constructive, but does not include voting rights held only as a director or trustee.

Conflict of interest. A "conflict of interest" arises where an individual is in a position where he or she is on both sides of an actual or potential transaction or other situation. A conflict of interest is not always contrary to law; often, this type of conflict is remedied through disclosure or consent.

Consideration. "Consideration" is one of the principal elements of an enforceable contract. Consideration is the reason one person contracts with another; the contracting party is motivated or impelled by the benefit to be derived from the contract (usually, goods or services), and the compensation to be received by the other person is that person's inducement to enter into the contract.

Constitutive document. A "constitutive document" is the document by which a *tax-exempt organization* is formed (constituted). This document is also referred to as the *articles of organization.*

Constructive ownership. "Constructive ownership" takes place when an item of property owned by a person is deemed by the law to be also owned by another person, for one or more purposes, where there is a defined relationship between the two persons. Rules of this nature are used to determine whether an entity is a *35 percent controlled entity*. There are two basic rules of this nature: (1) in instances involving corporations, indirect stockholdings are taken into account when they would be taken into account under the *related taxpayers constructive ownership rules* used in ascertaining losses, expenses, and interest with respect to transactions between related taxpayers (IRC § 4946(a)(3)); and (2) in instances involving partnerships or trusts, the ownership of profits or beneficial interests is determined in accordance with the related taxpayers constructive ownership rules (IRC § 4946(a)(4)).

Correction. The term "correction" means undoing an *excess benefit* to the extent possible and taking any additional measures necessary to place the *applicable tax-exempt organization* in a financial position not worse than that in which it would be if the *disqualified person* involved was dealing under the *highest fiduciary standards* (IRC § 4958(f)(6)).

Correction period. The term "correction period" means, with respect to a *taxable event*, the period beginning on the date on which the event occurs and ending ninety days after the date of mailing of a notice of deficiency (IRC § 6212), extended by any period in which a deficiency cannot be assessed and any other period that the IRS determines is *reasonable* (IRC § 4963(e)).

Disqualified person. A "disqualified person" is (1) a person who was, at any time during the five-year period ending on the date of the *excess benefit transaction* involved, in a position to exercise *substantial influence* over the affairs of the *applicable tax-exempt organization* involved (whether by virtue of being an *organization manager* or otherwise), (2) a *member of the family* of an individual described in the preceding category, and (3) an entity in which individuals described in the preceding two categories own more than 35 percent of an interest (a *35 percent controlled entity*) (IRC § 4958(f)(1)(A)-(C)).

Excess benefit. An "excess benefit" is the economic value of a benefit provided to a *disqualified person* by an *applicable tax-exempt organization* in an *excess benefit transaction* to the extent it exceeds the *consideration* received by the organization (IRC § 4958(c)(1)(B)).

Excess benefit transaction. The general definition of an "excess benefit transaction" is any transaction in which an economic benefit is provided by an *applicable tax-exempt organization* directly or indirectly to or for the use of any *disqualified person*, if the value of the economic benefit provided by the organization exceeds the value of the *consideration* (including the performance of services) received for providing the benefit (IRC § 4958(c)(1)(A)). An "excess benefit transaction" also includes any transaction in which the amount of any economic benefit provided to or for the use of a disqualified person is determined in whole or in part by the revenues of one or more activities of the organization but only if the transaction results in impermissible *private inurement* (IRC § 4958(c)(2)).

Fiduciary. A "fiduciary" is a person who has special responsibilities in connection with the administration, investment, and distribution of property, usually property belonging to someone else. This range of duties is termed "fiduciary responsibility."

Fiduciary responsibility. See *Fiduciary.*

First-tier tax. See *Initial excise tax.*

Form 990. See *Annual information return.*

Form 990-EZ. The "Form 990-EZ" is an *annual information return* that a *tax-exempt organization* may file in a year in which it has gross receipts of less than $100,000 and total assets of less than $250,000 at the end of the year.

Form 4720. The "Form 4720" is the return used to report liability for a variety of excise taxes in the *tax-exempt organizations* context, including those under the *intermediate sanctions* rules.

Fraternal organization. A "fraternal organization" is an organization that is *tax-exempt* because it is described in IRC § 501(c)(8) or (10). An organization of this nature provides various membership benefits; it may be based on the lodge system. This category of tax exemption is the subject of Chapter 34, § 4, of *Tax-Exempt Organizations.*

Harassment campaign. The term "harassment campaign" does not yet have a formal definition; it presumably will be defined in forthcoming federal tax regulations.

Independent board. An "independent board" is a board of trustees or board of directors of a *tax-exempt organization* that is comprised entirely of individuals who are not related (by a family or business relationship) to the individual who received from the organization an economic benefit that is under scrutiny.

Initial excise tax. The *intermediate sanctions* "initial excise tax" is a tax of 25 percent of the amount of an *excess benefit* received by a *disqualified person* from an *applicable tax-exempt organization* (IRC § 4958(a)(1)). This tax is also known as a "first-tier tax."

Intermediate sanctions. "Intermediate sanctions" are federal penalties, structured as excise taxes (IRC § 4958), which are imposed on *disqualified persons* who engage in *excess benefit transactions* with *applicable tax-exempt organizations,* and on *organization managers* who *knowingly* approve of such transactions. These sanctions are termed "intermediate" because they are on the spectrum of action by the IRS between doing nothing in the face of an economic abuse of an applicable tax-exempt organization and the drastic alternative of revocation of the organization's *tax-exempt* status.

Inure. The word "inure" means to cause to flow through something and become the possession of a person. It is used in the organizational setting to refer to the transfer of income or other resources to those who own or control the entity. For example, a for-profit corporation will earn a profit and, by declaring a dividend, will pass along a portion of that profit to other persons, who are stockholders in the corporation; this is known as *private inurement.*

Inurement, private. See *Private inurement.*

Knowing. An individual engages in a transaction "knowing" it to be an *excess benefit transaction* when he or she (1) had actual knowledge of sufficient facts so that, based solely on those facts, the transaction would involve an *excess benefit;* (2) was aware that the act, under the circumstances, may violate the *intermediate sanctions* rules; and (3) negligently failed to make *reasonable* attempts to ascertain whether the transaction involved an excess benefit, or was in fact aware that the transaction was an excess benefit one.

Member of the family. A "member of the family" means (1) spouses, ancestors, children, grandchildren, great grandchildren, and the spouses of children, grandchildren, and great grandchildren, and (2) the brothers and sisters (whether by the whole or half blood) of the individual, and their spouses (IRC § 4958(f)(4)).

Officer. An individual is an "officer" of a *tax-exempt organization* if he or she is (1) specifically so designated under the articles of incorporation, bylaws, or other *constitutive documents* of the organization, or (2) regularly exercises general authority to make administrative or policy decisions on behalf of the organization.

Organization manager. An "organization manager" is a trustee, director, or *officer* of an *applicable tax-exempt organization,* as well as an individual having powers or responsibilities similar to those of trustees, directors, or officers of the organization (IRC § 4958(f)(2)).

Presumption. A "presumption" is an inference drawn from a set of facts that leads to a conclusion regarding another set of facts or to a conclusion of law.

Private benefit doctrine. An organization cannot qualify as a *tax-exempt* charitable organization under the federal tax law if it violates the "private benefit doctrine." This doctrine, which is broader than and subsumes the *private inurement* doctrine, states that tax exemption on this basis is not available if the organization operates to benefit private interests to more than an insubstantial extent. This prohibition is not limited to situations where the benefits accrue to an organization's insiders with respect to it (as is the case with the private inurement doctrine). The law of private benefit is the subject of Chapter 13, § 7, of *Tax-Exempt Organizations.*

Private foundation. A "private foundation" is a type of charitable organization. The federal tax law *presumes* that a charitable organization is a private foundation (IRC § 509(a)); essentially, the presumption can be *rebutted* by a showing that the organization is a *public charity.* A private foundation generally has the following characteristics: (1) it is, as noted, a charitable entity; (2) it is funded, often in a single transaction (such as a major gift or bequest from an estate), from one source (such as an individual, family, or corporation); (3) its operating funds are in the form of investment income derived from investment of its assets (rather than an ongoing flow of contributions); and (4) it makes grants to other charitable organizations in furtherance of their purposes (rather than fund and conduct its own program). The law of private foundations is the subject of Chapters 16–18 of *Tax-Exempt Organizations.*

Private inurement. The doctrine of "private inurement" is the rule of the federal tax law that essentially differentiates nonprofit organizations from for-profit organizations. The doctrine forbids ways of causing the income or assets of *tax-exempt organizations* subject to the doctrine from flowing away from the organization and to one or more persons *(inuring),* who have some significant relationship with the organization (insiders), for their private purposes. Forms of private inurement include unreasonable compensation, unreasonable rental arrangements, unreasonable borrowing arrangements, unreasonable sales arrangements, and some involvements by tax-exempt organizations in joint ventures or partnerships. The law of private inurement is the subject of Chapter 13 of *Tax-Exempt Organizations.*

Public charity. A "public charity" is an organization that is *tax-exempt* because it is a charitable, educational, scientific, religious, or like organization (that is, is described in IRC § 501(c)(3)); this type of charitable organization is not (by reason of IRC § 509(a)) a *private foundation.* Public charities include churches, schools, hospitals, medical research organizations, *publicly supported charities,* and *supporting organizations*. The law of public charities is the subject of Chapter 17 of *Tax-Exempt Organizations.*

Publicly supported charity. There are two basic categories of charitable organizations that are not *private foundations* by reason of the fact that they are "publicly supported organizations." They are the donative publicly supported organization (IRC §§ 170(b)(1)(A)(vi) and 509(a)(1)) and the service provider publicly supported organization (IRC § 509(a)(2)). Both of these types of organizations must receive at least one-third of their total support in the form of public support (although the manner of calculating public support varies); generally, this calculation is made over a four-year measuring period. The law of publicly supported charities is the subject of Chapter 17, §§ 2–4, of *Tax-Exempt Organizations.*

Qualified first-tier tax. The *intermediate sanctions initial excise tax* is a "qualified first-tier tax," which means that the IRS has the authority to *abate* it.

Reasonable. Despite its widespread use in the law, the term "reasonable" eludes easy definition. It is often synonymous with "rational," being derived from the word "reason," which is a faculty of the mind enabling the individual to distinguish truth from falsehood and good from evil, and to deduce inferences from facts. When it is said that an *applicable tax-exempt organization* must confine its payments of compensation and other items (such as interest and rent) to levels that are "reasonable," what is meant is that the payments may not be excessive or immoderate (often termed "unreasonable").

Reasonable cause. The term "reasonable cause" is used to describe a range of circumstances as a result of which a person is excused from responsibility for a particular act (commission) or failure to act (omission). Although the application of this term is necessarily fact-specific and somewhat subjective, it can be said to mean a reliance on a set of facts and circumstances that seems at the time, to a person using average caution and care, to justify the course of action or inaction selected. Usually, an individual acts using "reasonable cause" if he or she has exercised his or her responsibility with respect to a *tax-exempt organization* with ordinary business care and prudence.

Rebuttable presumption. The term "rebuttable presumption" means a *presumption* as to the validity of one or more facts that will remain in place unless disproved or overridden (rebutted) by one or more other facts.

Related taxpayers constructive ownership rules. The "related taxpayers constructive ownership rules" require that (1) stock owned, directly or indirectly, by or for a corporation, partnership, estate, or trust be considered as being owned proportionately by or for its shareholders, partners, or beneficiaries; (2) an individual be considered as owning the stock owned, directly or indirectly, by or for the *members of* his or her *family;* (3) an individual owning (otherwise than by reason of the previous rule) any stock in a corporation be considered owning the stock owned, directly or indirectly, by or for his or her partner; and (4) stock *constructively owned* by a person by reason of the first of these rules be, for the purpose of applying all of these rules, treated as actually owned by that person (IRC § 267(c)). Stock constructively owned by an individual by reason of the second or third of these rules is not treated as owned by him or her for the purpose of again applying either of these rules in order to make another the constructive owner of the stock.

Revenue-sharing arrangement. A "revenue-sharing arrangement" is a financial arrangement by which a person receives a payment from a tax-exempt organization based on the organization's income, such as a commission or like percentage-based compensation.

Second-tier tax. See *Additional excise tax.*

Self-dealing. The term "self-dealing" is used to describe a transaction where a *fiduciary* acquires or makes use of property, which belongs to the person as to whom the fiduciary stands in a fiduciary relationship, for his, her, or its benefit. In the *private foundation* context, a variety of transactions between foundations and disqualified persons are considered self-dealing (IRC § 4941). These rules, as amplified by tax regulations, revenue rulings, private letter rulings, and court opinions, have proven to be a formidable barrier to inappropriate arrangements between a private foundation and those closely associated with it. In many ways, these self-dealing rules are a codification of important elements of the *private inurement* proscription. The self-dealing rules are the subject of Chapter 20 of *Tax-Exempt Organizations.*

Social club. A "social club" is an organization that is *tax-exempt* because it is described in IRC § 501(c)(7). This type of club is organized for pleasure, recreation, and other nonprofitable purposes. The law of social clubs is the subject of Chapter 30 of *Tax-Exempt Organizations.*

Social welfare organization. A "social welfare organization" is an organization that is *tax-exempt* because it is described in IRC

§ 501(c)(4). As the name indicates, this type of organization must engage in "social welfare" (such as civic) activities; these activities must be those that benefit a community. Social welfare organizations often engage in advocacy, particularly lobbying, activities. The law of social welfare organizations is the subject of Chapter 28 of *Tax-Exempt Organizations*.

Statute of limitations. A "statute of limitations" is a law that sets a period of time within which a person must institute a legal proceeding (litigation, an administrative hearing, or some other action to enforce a right) or else be barred from asserting the claim.

Substantial influence. The term "substantial influence" does not yet have a formal definition; it presumably will be defined in forthcoming federal tax regulations.

Supporting organizations. One of the ways in which a charitable organization can avoid being classified as a *private foundation* is to constitute a "supporting organization" (IRC § 509(a)(3)). This type of organization is sufficiently related to one or more organizations that are *public charities* so that the requisite degree of public control and involvement is considered present. A supporting organization must be organized and operated exclusively for the benefit of, to perform the functions of, or to carry out the purposes of, one or more public charities. It must be operated, supervised, or controlled by or in connection with one or more public charities. Thus, the relationship must be one of three types: (1) operated, supervised, or controlled by; (2) supervised or controlled in connection with; or (3) operated in connection with.

Taxable event. The term "taxable event" means any act or failure to act giving rise to liability for tax by reason of violation of rules such as those for *intermediate sanctions* (IRC § 4963(c)).

Taxable period. The "taxable period" is the period beginning with the date on which an *excess benefit transaction* occurred and ending on the earliest of the date of mailing of a notice of deficiency with respect to the *initial excise tax* or the date on which the initial excise tax is assessed (IRC § 4958(f)(5)).

Tax-exempt. The term "tax-exempt" means excused from the requirement of payment of federal income taxes (IRC § 501(a)).

Tax-exempt organization. An organization is a "tax-exempt organization" when it is exempt from one or more federal, state, or local taxes; it is an organization with a tax exemption. Usually, the term "tax-exempt organization" is applied to an organization that is exempt from an income tax. The federal tax law specifically provides for exemption from federal income taxation (IRC § 501(a)) and enumerates in one provision (IRC § 501(c)(1)–(27)) most of the organizations that are exempt from tax. The other tax exemption provisions are IRC §§ 501(d) and 526–529.

Taxpayer Bill of Rights 2. The "Taxpayer Bill of Rights 2" is the name of the tax legislation that includes the *intermediate sanctions* rules (P.L. 104–168, 104th Cong., 2d Sess. (1996), 110 Stat. 1452).

35 percent controlled entity. A "35 percent controlled entity" can be a corporation in which one or more *disqualified persons* own more than 35 percent of the total *combined voting power,* a partnership in which one or more disqualified persons own more than 35 percent of the profits interest, or a trust or estate in which one or more disqualified persons own more than 35 percent of the beneficial interest (IRC § 4958(f)(3)(A)).

Veterans' organization. A "veterans' organization" is an organization that is *tax-exempt* because it is described in IRC § 501(c)(19). For the most part, a veterans' organization is tax-exempt because it is a post or other organization of past or present members of the armed forces of the United States or an auxiliary unit or society of, or a trust or foundation for, any such post or other organization. This category of tax exemption is the subject of Chapter 34, § 10, of *Tax-Exempt Organizations.*

Widely available. The term "widely available" does not yet have a formal definition; it presumably will be defined in forthcoming federal tax regulations.

Selected
Bibliography

The following listing, presented in reverse chronological order, references articles focusing on intermediate sanctions that have appeared over the past few years.

Hopkins, "Intermediate Sanctions: Understanding the New Tax Penalties on Nonprofit Managers," 1 *Nonprofit Management Rev.* (No. 1) 60 (Spring 1997).

"Intermediate Sanctions: Former IRS Official Explains the New Law's Effect on Colleges," 15 *Exempt Organization Tax Review* (No. 3) 365 (Dec. 1996).

"Academic Medical Centers Must Be Aware of New Sanctions Criteria, Owens Says," *Daily Tax Report* (No. 235) G-10 (Dec. 6, 1996).

"Owens Urges Reason in Dealing with Intermediate Sanctions," 4 *EOTR Weekly* (No. 2) 1 (Oct. 7, 1996).

Suhrke, "Is Friendly Fire Killing Charity? How Intermediate Are IRS's New Powers?," XXIX *The Philanthropy Monthly* (No. 7) 5 (Sept. 1996).

"Intermediate Sanctions Enacted: Implications for Fund-Raising," III *Fund-Raising Regulation Report* (No. 5) 1 (Sept./Oct. 1996).

"For Intermediate Sanctions Guidance, Look to Statute and Legislative History," 4 *EOTR Weekly* (No. 1) 1 (Sept. 30, 1996).

"Guidance on Intermediate Sanctions on 'Fast Track,' Owens Says," 4 *EOTR Weekly* (No. 1) 2 (Sept. 30, 1996).

"New Intermediate Sanctions Present Many Questions, Few Answers," 72 *Tax Notes* 1727 (Sept. 30, 1996).

"IRS Official Pledges 'Reasonable' Enforcement of Intermediate Sanctions," *Daily Tax Report* (No. 187) G-1 (Sept. 26, 1996).

183

"Panelists Sound Warning on Intermediate Sanctions," 3 *EOTR Weekly* (No. 13) 99 (Sept. 23, 1996).

"IRS Announces Due Date for Excise Taxes on Excess Benefit Transactions under 'T2'," *Daily Tax Report* (No. 178) G-2 (Sept. 13, 1996).

Davis and Thomas, "Exempt Organizations Should Support Intermediate Sanctions Legislation," 8 *Journal of Taxation of Exempt Organizations* (No. 2) 51 (Sept./Oct. 1996).

Crozier, "Intermediate Sanctions Will Affect Exempt Organizations' Hiring and Compensation Policies," 8 *Journal of Taxation of Exempt Organizations* (No. 2) 61 (Sept./Oct. 1996).

"Intermediate Sanctions Portions of H.R. 2337, Taxpayer Bill of Rights 2," 14 *Exempt Organization Tax Review* (No. 3) 423 (Sept. 1996).

"Intermediate Sanctions Become Law," XIII *The Nonprofit Counsel* (No. 9) 1 (Sept. 1996).

Schoenfeld and Repass, "'Intermediate Sanctions'—Issues, Pitfalls, and Protective Measures," *Tax Notes* 1033 (Aug. 19, 1996).

"EO Input on Intermediate Sanctions Wanted, Treasury Official Says," 72 *Tax Notes* 809 (Aug. 12, 1996).

Davis, Jr., and Thomas, "New Penalties Unlikely to Cut Abuse at Charities," VIII *Chronicle of Philanthropy* (No. 21) 52 (Aug. 8, 1996).

Peregrine, Nilles, and Palmer, "Complying with the New Intermediate Sanctions Law," 14 *Exempt Organization Tax Review* (No. 2) 245 (Aug. 1996).

Hopkins, "Legislation Would Force Groups to Re-Examine Employee Pay," 14 *Kansas City Business Journal* (No. 45) 18 (July 26–Aug. 1, 1996).

"Tax-Exempts Should Examine Compensation Packages," *Daily Tax Report* (No. 145) I-1 (July 29, 1996).

"Intermediate Sanctions Move Closer to Reality," 72 *Tax Notes* 397 (July 22, 1996).

"Senate Passes Taxpayer Bill of Rights with Intermediate Sanctions Provision," 5 *Health Law Reporter* 1083 (July 18, 1996).

"Intermediate Sanctions: Where We Are," XIII *The Nonprofit Counsel* (No. 7) 1 (July 1996).

Beers, "New Legislation Increases Scrutiny of Not-For-Profit Compensation," XXIX *The Philanthropy Monthly* (No. 5) 5 (June 1996).

"What the Intermediate Sanctions Law Provides," XXIX *The Philanthropy Monthly* (No. 5) 10 (June 1996).

"Intermediate Sanctions Pass House," XIII *The Nonprofit Counsel* (No. 6) 1 (June 1996).

"IRS Has High Hopes for Intermediate Sanctions, Owens Says," 2 *EOTR Weekly* (No. 12) 74 (June 17, 1996).

"Intermediate Sanctions Promptly Resurrected," XIII *The Nonprofit Counsel* (No. 5) 1 (May 1996).

"Intermediate Sanctions Face Uncertain Fate in Senate," 71 *Tax Notes* 571 (Apr. 29, 1996).

"Intermediate Sanctions Proposals Emerge from White House, Capitol Hill," 13 *Exempt Organization Tax Review* (No. 4) 525 (Apr. 1996).

"JCT Reports on Taxpayer Bill of Rights 2 Legislation," 13 *Exempt Organization Tax Review* (No. 4) 687 (Apr. 1996).

"Statutory Language and Treasury Report for Exempt Organization Tax Provisions in President Clinton's Proposed Fiscal 1997 Budget," 13 *Exempt Organization Tax Review* (No. 4) 691 (Apr. 1996).

"Intermediate Sanctions—The Rationale, the Proposals, and the Legislation," 13 *Exempt Organization Tax Review* (No. 4) 560 (Apr. 1996).

"Intermediate Sanctions Measure Clears House Committee," 3 *EOTR Weekly* 1 (Apr. 1, 1996).

"Sen. Inouye Renews Request for Intermediate Sanctions Modifications," 13 *Exempt Organization Tax Review* (No. 3) 497 (Mar. 1996).

Brier, "A Critique of the Intermediate Sanctions Proposal Contained in the Revenue Reconciliation Act of 1995, H.R. 2491," 13 *Exempt Organization Tax Review* (No. 2) 211 (Feb. 1996).

"White House Remains Committed to Intermediate Sanctions for EOs," 13 *Exempt Organization Tax Review* (No. 2) 201 (Feb. 1996).

"Substantiation Rules, Intermediate Sanctions Dominate EOs in 1995," 13 *Exempt Organization Tax Review* (No. 1) 5 (Jan. 1996).

Jones, "Intermediate Sanctions, Revenue Sharing, and Too Many EOs Anyway," 13 *Exempt Organization Tax Review* (No. 1) 67 (Jan. 1996).

"Congress Passes Tax Legislation, Which Is Vetoed; Negotiations for New Package Continue," XIII *The Nonprofit Counsel* (No. 1) 1 (Jan. 1996).

"Intermediate Sanctions Would Affect Ability of Organizations to Hire Top People, Attorney Asserts," 12 *Exempt Organization Tax Review* (No. 5) 1108 (Nov. 1995).

"Intermediate Sanctions: On the Road to Enactment," XII *The Nonprofit Counsel* (No. 11) 1 (Nov. 1995).

"JCT Suggests Intermediate Sanction Guidelines for Excess Compensation," 12 *Exempt Organization Tax Review* (No. 4) 705 (Oct. 1995).

"New Version of Intermediate Sanctions Proposed by Treasury," XII *The Nonprofit Counsel* (No. 10) 1 (Oct. 1995).

"Latest Intermediate Sanctions Proposal Contains New Twists," 12 *Exempt Organization Tax Review* (No. 3) 531 (Sept. 1995).

"Faber Says Intermediate Sanctions Proposal May Affect Indisputably Bona Fide Organizations," 12 *Exempt Organization Tax Review* (No. 3) 685 (Sept. 1995).

"Samuels Submits White House Intermediate Sanctions Proposal," 12 *Exempt Organization Tax Review* (No. 2) 510 (Aug. 1995).

"Faber Favors Intermediate Sanctions Legislation," 12 *Exempt Organization Tax Review* (No. 2) 502 (Aug. 1995).

Suhrke, "Can Process Routine Justify the Trespass of Intermediate Sanctions?" XXVII *The Philanthropy Monthly* (No. I) 13 (June 1995).

"Treasury Summarizes Legislative Status of Intermediate Sanctions," 11 *Exempt Organization Tax Review* (No. 5) 1138 (May 1995).

"Fremont-Smith on Intermediate Sanctions," 11 *Exempt Organization Tax Review* (No. 4) 695 (Apr. 1995).

"Better Late Than Never—Intermediate Sanctions Provisions Contained in the House Offer to the Senate with Respect to GATT," 11 *Exempt Organization Tax Review* (No. 4) 881 (Apr. 1995).

"Bromberg Raises Questions on Hermann Hospital, Intermediate Sanctions," 11 *Exempt Organization Tax Review* (No. 1) 20 (Jan. 1995).

"Intermediate Sanctions for EOs Discussed at Tax Program," 10 *Exempt Organization Tax Review* (No. 6) 1269 (Dec. 1994).

"Commentator Says Safe Harbor for Intermediate Sanctions Is Needed," 10 *Exempt Organization Tax Review* (No. 3) 794 (Sept. 1994).

"Intermediate Sanctions May Help Fund Trade Agreement," XI *The Nonprofit Counsel* (No. 9) 1 (Sept. 1994).

ABA Committee on Exempt Organizations, "Comments on Compliance with the Tax Laws by Public Charities" [a.k.a. "Intermediate Sanctions White Paper"], reprinted in 10 *Exempt Organization Tax Review* (No. 1) 74 (July 1994).

Boisture, "Proposals Affecting Tax-Exempt Health Care Organizations in the Ways and Means and Finance Committee Health Care Bills," 10 *Exempt Organization Tax Review* (No. 1) 109 (July 1994).

Fremont-Smith, "Current Proposals for Public Charity Intermediate Sanctions," 10 *Exempt Organization Tax Review* (No. 1) 115 (July 1994).

"June 13 Letter from Independent Sector to W&M Chairman Sam Gibbons," 10 *Exempt Organization Tax Review* (No. 1) 14 (July 1994).

"Proposed Amendment to Chairman's Mark Submitted by Six Health Care Organizations," 10 *Exempt Organization Tax Review* (No. 1) 15 (July 1994).

"Fund-Raising Group Comments on Intermediate Sanctions Proposal," 10 *Exempt Organization Tax Review* (No. 1) 216 (July 1994).

"Reform Tax-Exempts Before Tackling Health Care," 10 *Exempt Organization Tax Review* (No. 1) 11 (July 1994).

"Council on Foundations Supports Intermediate Sanctions," 10 *Exempt Organization Tax Review* (No. 1) 209 (July 1994).

"Tax-Exempt Health Care Providers Should Be Getting Nervous," 10 *Exempt Organization Tax Review* (No. 1) 6 (July 1994).

"Health Care Reform Mark Includes Forms of Intermediate Sanctions," XI *The Nonprofit Counsel* (No. 7) 1 (July 1994).

"N.Y.C. Bar Supports Intermediate Sanctions on Exempt Groups," 9 *Exempt Organization Tax Review* (No. 6) 1417 (June 1994).

"Brorby Writes Treasury Concerning the Proposed Intermediate Sanctions," 9 *Exempt Organization Tax Review* (No. 6) 1409 (June 1994).

"Business Coalition Supports Intermediate Sanctions Proposal," 9 *Exempt Organization Tax Review* (No. 6) 1410 (June 1994).

"W&M Oversight Subcommittee Report on 'Reforms to Improve the Tax Rules Governing Public Charities,'" 9 *Exempt Organization Tax Review* (No. 6) 1219 (June 1994).

"Troyer Praises Intermediate Sanctions Proposal," 9 *Exempt Organization Tax Review* (No. 6) 1404 (June 1994).

"Ways and Means Panel Reports on Intermediate Sanctions for EOs," 9 *Exempt Organization Tax Review* (No. 6) 1217 (June 1994).

"Treasury's Mike Schultz Reviews Intermediate Sanctions Proposals," 9 *Exempt Organization Tax Review* (No. 6) 1201 (June 1994).

"Intermediate Sanctions Hot Topic at Georgetown EO Conference," 63 *Tax Notes* 643 (May 9, 1994).

"Independent Sector Supports Treasury's EO Compliance Proposals," 9 *Exempt Organization Tax Review* (No. 5) 1157 (May 1994).

"Former EO Committee Chairs Voice Intermediate Sanctions Concerns," 9 *Exempt Organization Tax Review* (No. 5) 1165 (May 1994).

"Treasury Proposes 'Intermediate Sanctions' Plan, New Disclosure Rules," XI *The Nonprofit Counsel* (No. 5) 1 (May 1994).

Boisture and Cerny, "Treasury Proposes Intermediate Sanctions on Public Charities and Section 501(c)(4) Organizations," 9 *Exempt Organization Tax Review* (No. 4) 799 (Apr. 1994).

"Schultz and Vance Outline Plans for Intermediate Sanctions," 9 *Exempt Organization Tax Review* (No. 4) 732 (Apr. 1994).

ABA Tax Section Exempt Organizations Committee, "Panel Two: Proposals for Intermediate Sanctions for Charitable Organizations," 9 *Exempt Organization Tax Review* (No. 3) 536 (Mar. 1994).

"Administration Proposes Excise Tax To End Abuse by Exempt Entities," *Daily Tax Report* (No. 51) G-4, L-1 (Mar. 17, 1994).

"Transcript of the March 16, 1994, Hearing of the Oversight Subcommittee of the House Ways and Means Committee," reprinted in 9 *Exempt Organization Tax Review* (No. 3) 763 (Mar. 1994).

"Independent Sector Position on Possible Legislation Related to Performance and Accountability of Public Charities," 9 *Exempt Organization Tax Review* (No. 1) 151 (Jan. 1994).

Peregrine and Broccolo, "Stark Introduces Exempt Organizations 'Intermediate Sanctions' Legislation," 9 *Exempt Organization Tax Review* (No. 1) 131 (Jan. 1994).

"Treasury's Testimony on Tax Provisions in Health Security Act at W&M Subcommittee Hearing," 9 *Exempt Organization Tax Review* (No. 1) 84 (Jan. 1994) (contains statement of Maurice B. Foley, Deputy Tax Legislative Counsel (Tax Legislation), Department of the Treasury, regarding Intermediate Sanctions and Health Care Organizations).

"Rep. Stark Proposes Intermediate Sanctions Legislation," XI *The Nonprofit Counsel* (No. 1) 3 (Jan. 1994).

Bromberg, "Intermediate Sanctions," outline presented at the National Health Lawyers Association Conference on Tax Issues in Nonprofit Healthcare Organizations, 1994.

Boisture and Cerny, "Second Oversight Subcommittee Hearing Explores Need for Intermediate Sanctions and More Disclosure," 93 *Tax Notes Today* 188 (Sept. 10, 1993).

"House Subcommittee Launches Hearings on Public Charities; Focus on Inurement," X *The Nonprofit Counsel* (No. 7) 1 (July 1993).

"Bill Introduced to Extend Self-Dealing Rules to Health Organizations," IX *The Nonprofit Counsel* (No. 3) 7 (Mar. 1992).

Index